The MRCOG:
A Guide to the
Examination

D1458760

The MRCOG:
A Guide
to the
Examination

Third edition

Edited by

William L Ledger

and

Michael G Murphy

Series Editor: **Jenny M Higham**

Published by the **RCOG Press** at the Royal College of Obstetricians and Gynaecologists, 27 Sussex Place, Regent's Park, London NW1 4RG

www.rcog.org.uk

Registered charity no. 213280

First published 2008

Disclaimer
Care has been taken to provide accurate and up-to-date information. However, this is not guaranteed. No responsibility will be accepted for any loss, damage or expense resulting from the use of this information. The information is not meant to be authoritative. The publisher can give no guarantee for information and application thereof contained in this book. In every individual case the respective user must check its accuracy by consulting the relevant authorities.

ISBN 978-1-904752-57-8

Cover illustration: Dr Helen Bolton, MRCOG Prize Medallist, receiving her medal from the President, Professor Sabaratnam Arulkumaran FRCOG

RCOG Editor: Jane Moody
Design/typesetting: Karl Harrington, FiSH Book, London
Index: Liza Furnival, Medical Indexing Ltd
Printed in the UK by Latimer Trend & Co. Ltd, Estover Road, Plymouth PL6 7PL

Contents

Foreword

An updated guide to the MRCOG examination, in the user friendly and compact volume of the MRCOG and Beyond series will be a 'must buy' for many candidates. It is authoritatively written by those with current or very recent involvement in the examinations and hence the relevance and accuracy of the information it contains.

Examinations change with time and understanding the newer question formats is vital, particularly as they may be unfamiliar to candidates from their own undergraduate days.

Learn from it and good luck!

Professor Jenny M Higham
Head of Undergraduate Medicine, Imperial College London

Preface

This book is designed as a guide for candidates preparing for the Part 1 and Part 2 Membership (MRCOG) examinations of the Royal College of Obstetricians and Gynaecologists. During the past few years, a large number of changes have been made to College examinations, some of which have been introduced in response to the requirements of a new statutory body, the Postgraduate Medical Education and Training Board (PMETB). For example, in August 2007, a new Specialty Training and Education Programme in Obstetrics and Gynaecology was introduced in the UK. This has necessitated the development by the College of a new curriculum which, in turn, has prompted the introduction of a new syllabus for both the Part 1 and Part 2 MRCOG examinations. Details of the new curriculum and syllabuses and their impact upon the examinations are included in this volume. There is also a chapter on the significance of the Membership examination in a global context and the reasons for its continued popularity among candidates.

The book is divided into chapters which focus on the individual components of the Membership examination. The authors have been closely involved in planning and implementing the recent changes to the various components of the examination. Concepts such as the standard setting and blueprinting of examinations are explained in detail, in addition to accounts of newly introduced formats such as extended matching questions (EMQs), and the evolution of the essay questions into short-answer questions (SAQs) in Part 2.

All the recent changes to the Membership examination have been made with the express purpose of improving the validity and reliability of the examination as a whole. We are confident that this has been the case: a contention that was endorsed by PMETB's formal approval of the College's examination and assessment processes in June 2007.

Most importantly, this book is intended to assist candidates with their revision for the examinations and to provide helpful information on how to obtain a pass. We hope that you will find it useful.

William L Ledger
Michael G Murphy

About the authors

Meghna Datta MB BS
Specialist Registrar
Jessop Wing, Royal Hallamshire Hospital,
Sheffield

Alison N Fiander DM FRCOG
Professor of Obstetrics and Gynaecology
Wales College of Medicine, Cardiff
University, Cardiff, Wales
Chair, Part 1 MRCOG Sub-committee
2005–2008

Paul P Fogarty MD FRCOG
Consultant Obstetrician and Gynaecologist
Ulster Hospital, Belfast
Member, Part 2 MRCOG Essay Papers
Sub-committee 2001–2004
Chair, Part 2 MRCOG SAQ
Sub-committee 2004–2007

Paul D Hodges BA PhD
Deputy to Head of Examination Department
Royal College of Obstetricians and
Gynaecologists

**Tony A Hollingworth FRCS(Ed) MBA
PhD FRCOG**
Consultant Obstetrician and Gynaecologist
Whipps Cross University NHS Trust,
London
Member, Part 2 MRCOG Oral Assessment
Sub-committee 2001–2004
Chair, Part 2 MRCOG Oral Assessment
Sub-committee 2004–2007

Justin C Konje MD MRCOG
Professor of Obstetrics and Gynaecology
University of Leicester
Member, Part 2 MRCOG MCQ
Sub-committee 2001–2004
Chair, Part 2 MRCOG MCQ
Sub-committee 2004–2007

William L Ledger MA DPhil FRCOG
Professor of Obstetrics and Gynaecology
University of Sheffield
Chair, Examination and Assessment
Committee
Chair, Part 1 MCQ Sub-committee
2002–2005

Michael G Murphy MA MSc PhD
*Director of Education and Head of
Examination Department*
Royal College of Obstetricians and
Gynaecologists

Ian N Ramsay MRCOG
Consultant Obstetrician and Gynaecologist
Stirling Royal Infirmary, Stirling, Scotland
Member, Part 2 MRCOG EMQ
Sub-committee 2003–2005
Chair, Part 2 MRCOG EMQ
Sub-committee 2005–2008

Wendy MN Reid FRCOG
Consultant Obstetrician and Gynaecologist
Royal Free Hampstead NHS Trust,
London
Chair, Part 2 MRCOG EMQ
Sub-committee 2003–2005

Series Editor:
Jenny M Higham
MD FRCOG FFFP ILTM
*Head of Undergraduate Medicine/
Consultant Gynaecologist*
Faculty of Medicine, Imperial College
London

1 Curriculum and syllabus

The concept of curriculum

The word *curriculum* in Latin originally meant a race, course or lap, in its literal sense, and secondarily, in its figurative meaning, a course or career – hence, *curriculum vitae* meaning the course of one's life, or career. In English, 'curriculum' has come to mean the course of study offered by an educational institution. However, as with most things in education, there is no agreed definition of 'curriculum', although it is generally accepted that 'curriculum' is not the same as 'syllabus'. In this chapter, we look more closely at the terms 'curriculum' and 'syllabus' as they relate to the MRCOG examination and consider the merits of these concepts to candidates for the examination.

In its survey of the different types of curricula mentioned in the educational literature, the Postgraduate Medical Education and Training Board (PMETB) notes the following varieties:

The curriculum on paper	The statement of purpose, aims, content, experiences, materials; also known as the 'planned' or 'formal' curriculum.
The curriculum in action	The way in which the curriculum on paper is put into practice; also known as the 'received' curriculum.
The curriculum learners' experience	What learners do, how they study, what they believe they should be doing, and so on; the 'informal' curriculum.
The hidden curriculum	the behaviours, knowledge and performances that learners infer to be important.[1]

According to PMETB, any curriculum is based explicitly or implicitly on a model of how the relevant group learns. In the case of postgraduate medicine, individual trainees will construct their own version of the curriculum based on their own needs and opportunities and the relevant model of curriculum will include elements of:

• learning at formal, timetabled and protected events
• self-directed and independent study
• learning in the workplace.[2]

Taking into account all of these considerations, PMETB has adopted the following comprehensive definition of curriculum:

> 'A statement of the intended aims and objectives, content, experiences, outcomes and processes of an educational programme including:
>
> ○ a description of the training structure (entry requirements, length and organisation of the programme including its flexibilities, and assessment system)
> ○ a description of expected methods of learning, teaching, feedback and supervision.
>
> The curriculum should cover both generic professional and specialty specific areas.
>
> The syllabic content of the curriculum should be stated in terms of what knowledge, skills attitudes and expertise the learner will achieve.'[3]

A new curriculum in obstetrics and gynaecology

In 2004, the RCOG established a Curriculum Group, comprised of experienced consultants and educationalists and charged with the task of writing a new Curriculum in Obstetrics and Gynaecology as the basis for a new specialty training programme. This new curriculum was approved by PMETB in December 2006, in time for the national launch of the new Specialty Training and Education Programme in Obstetrics and Gynaecology in August 2007 (Figure 1.1).

The Curriculum represents the specialty training programme in obstetrics and gynaecology from Specialty Training Year 1 (ST1) to ST7. The programme is divided into three sections: basic, intermediate and advanced training. Although these sections appear as a continuous period of 7 years, it is important to note that the programme is competency-based rather than time-based. This means that a trainee's progress is determined by the attainment of the various competencies of the programme, with some trainees achieving these at a faster rate than

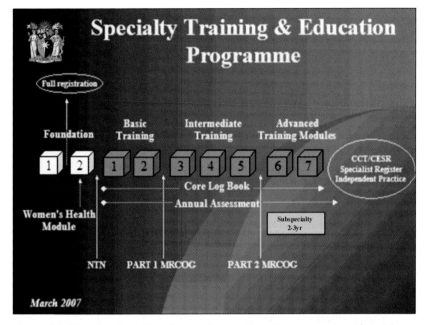

Specialty Training & Education Programme

Full registration

Foundation — Basic Training — Intermediate Training — Advanced Training Modules

1 2 1 2 3 4 5 6 7

CCT/CESR
Specialist Register
Independent Practice

Core Log Book
Annual Assessment

Women's Health Module

Subspecialty 2-3yr

NTN   PART 1 MRCOG   PART 2 MRCOG

March 2007

Figure 1.1. The Specialty Training and Education Programme in Obstetrics and Gynaecology launched in August 2007

others. The Curriculum contains a mission statement concerning the high-level purpose of the training programme, which sets out the parameters for learning. Accordingly, the Curriculum aims to develop a profession based on skills, with transparent professional standards and outcomes, benchmarked against the General Medical Council's document Good Medical Practice (GMP) under the following seven headings:[4]

i   Good clinical care
ii   Maintaining good medical practice
iii   Relationships with patients
iv   Working with colleagues
v   Teaching and training
vi   Probity
vii   Health.

The Curriculum therefore enables prospective candidates to see the breadth of the profession before applying to join it. Moreover, it develops a professional model that is reflexive, collective, developmental and process-orientated. Most importantly, the Curriculum acts as a reflection of the profession in terms of the standards expected in assessments. This, in turn, enables patients to see the standard of care that they can expect from the profession. Hence, it allows questions to be asked in the public domain in the context of the published curriculum.

The RCOG Core Curriculum is divided into 19 modules:

Module 1   Basic Clinical Skills

Module 2   Teaching, Appraisal and Assessment

Module 3   Information Technology, Clinical Governance and Research

Module 4   Ethics and Legal Issues

Module 5   Core Surgical Skills

Module 6   Postoperative Care

Module 7   Surgical Procedures

Module 8   Antenatal Care

Module 9   Maternal Medicine

Module 10   Management of Labour

Module 11   Management of Delivery

Module 12   Postpartum Problems (The Puerperium)

Module 13   Gynaecological Problems

Module 14   Subfertility

Module 15   Women's Sexual and Reproductive Health

Module 16   Early Pregnancy Care

Module 17   Gynaecological Oncology

Module 18   Urogynaecology and Pelvic Floor Problems

Module 19   Professional Development.

These modules were selected as representing the core subjects required in the preparation of trainees for the profession of obstetrics and gynaecology. They were based upon the sequence of topics which appeared in the Core Logbook produced by the College in July 2002. The complete Core Curriculum may be accessed on the College website under the section entitled Education.

Each module of the Curriculum is presented in the same general format (Figure 1.2), beginning with a set of learning outcomes. These outcomes are followed by a series of subtopics, each of which is analysed by five columns with the headings: Knowledge criteria, Clinical competency, Professional skills and attitudes, Training support and Evidence/assessment.

Curriculum Module 9: Maternal Medicine

Learning Outcomes:

- To understand and demonstrate appropriate knowledge, skills and attitudes in relation to maternal medicine.

Knowledge criteria	Clinical competency	Professional skills and attitudes	Training support	Evidence/assessment
- Understand the epidemiology, aetiology, pathophysiology, clinical characteristics, prognostic features and management of: ■ hypertension ■ kidney disease ■ heart disease ■ liver disease ■ circulatory disorders ■ disorders of carbohydrate metabolism ■ other endocrinopathies ■ gastrointestinal disorders ■ pulmonary diseases ■ connective tissue diseases ■ bone and joint disorders ■ psychiatric disorders ■ infectious diseases ■ neurological diseases - maternal complications due to pregnancy	- Diagnose, investigate and manage, with direct supervision: ■ pregnancy-induced hypertension ■ thromboembolism ■ impaired glucose tolerance ■ insulin-dependent diabetes ■ essential hypertension ■ kidney disease ■ liver disease ■ maternal haemoglobinopathy ■ coagulation disorders ■ acute abdominal pain ■ asthma ■ inflammatory bowel disease ■ intercurrent infection ■ psychological disorders ■ infectious disease ■ epilepsy - endocrinopathies	- Have the ability to recognise the normal from the abnormal - Develop the skills to competently formulate a list of differential diagnoses - Have the skills to request the relevant investigations to support the differential diagnoses - Competently demonstrate the skills to formulate a management plan - Have the ability to implement a plan of management and modify if necessary - Develop the skills to liaise effectively with colleagues in other disciplines, both clinical and nonclinical	- Local and regional courses - Attendance at medical disorders antenatal clinic - StratOG.net: Maternal Medicine e-tutorials - Useful websites: ■ **www.nice.org.uk** ■ **www.rcog.org.uk** ■ **www.sign.ac.uk** ■ **www.show.scot.nhs.uk/ spcerh** ■ **www.bmfms.org.uk**	- Logbook - Reflective diary - MRCOG Part 2 - Case reports - Audit projects

Figure 1.2. Example of format common to all Curriculum modules

Each module contains specific training targets, ranging from obser-vation (seeing a procedure) through direct supervision to independent practice. The first three columns represent the syllabic content of the curriculum. These clearly indicate the knowledge, skills, attitudes and expertise required by trainees. As in the example shown of Module 9, an appendix providing more detailed information to help trainees may supplement the Knowledge criteria (Figure 1.3).

The fourth column states where trainees can access the necessary training support in acquiring the relevant knowledge and competencies and the final column indicates the evidence of attainment and the means of assessment. The successful completion of each stage of train-ing will be dependent upon satisfactory performance in examinations and workplace-based assessments. These will include mini-clinical evaluation (mini-CEX), case-based discussion (CbD), multi-source feedback (MSF) and objective structured assessments of technical skills (OSATS). These assessments focus upon the acquisition of core surgical and complex interventional procedures commonly associated with obstetric and gynaecological practice. It is a requirement of PMETB that specific assessment methods should:[4]

(a)   have appropriate content and methods

(b)   be valid

(c)   be reliable

(d)   be based on evidence

(e)   be assessed against best practice in other settings and other countries.

The Curriculum is thus designed to be maximally transparent and helpful to trainees in providing comprehensive information and guid-ance concerning both the content and the means of assessment of their training programme. Thus, it is possible to see at a glance exactly which topics in obstetrics and gynaecology must be mastered and to what level of skill. At the end of each module there is a summary of the skills required for each module, together with a colour-coded chart indicating the required level of competence to be attained: basic, inter-mediate or advanced (Figure 1.4).

The Curriculum is modular and will change over time in parallel with new scientific discoveries and changes in clinical practice. The core knowledge of obstetrics and gynaecology will also change, but more slowly, and may continue in modules which differ from those at present, such as stem cell science and gene therapy. A quote from

Understand the epidemiology, aetiology, pathophysiology, clinical characteristics, prognostic features and management of:

Hypertension:
- Definitions
- Aetiological theories
- Organ involvement (mother, fetus)
- Diagnosis
- Drug therapy

Kidney disease:
- Urinary tract infection
- Pyelonephritis
- Glomerulonephritides
- Nephrotic syndrome
- Tubular necrosis
- Cortical necrosis
- Transplantation

Pulmonary diseases:
- Asthma
- Infection
- Embolism
- Aspiration syndrome

Neurological disorders:
- Epilepsy
- Cerebrovascular disease
- Multiple sclerosis
- Migraine
- Neuropathies
- Myasthenia gravis
- Paraplegia

Bone and joint disorders:
- Backache
- Symphyseal separation
- Metabolic bone disease
- Neoplasms (benign and malignant):
- Genital tract
- Breast
- Other

Psychiatric disorders:
- Manic depressive disorders
- Psychoneurosis
- Puerperal disorders (blues, depression)
- Mood disorders
- Schizophrenia
- Reaction to pregnancy loss

Gastrointestinal disorders:
- Nausea
- Vomiting
- Hyperemesis
- Gastric reflux
- Abdominal pain
- Appendicitis
- Inflammatory bowel disease

Intestinal obstruction

Heart disease:
- Congenital
- Rheumatic
- Ischaemic
- Cardiomyopathy
- Heart failure

Liver disease:
- Cholestasis
- Hepatitis
- Acute fatty degeneration

Circulatory disorders:
- Anaemia
- Sickle cell disease
- Thalassaemias
- Coagulation defects
- Thrombocytopenias
- Thromboembolism
- Transfusion
- Replacement of blood constituents
- Varicose veins (legs, vulva, haemorrhoids)

Connective tissue diseases:
- Systemic lupus erythematosus
- Rheumatoid arthritis
- Immunosupressant drugs

Disorders of carbohydrate metabolism:
- Diagnosis
- Type 1 and type 2 diabetes
- Hazards (maternal, fetal, neonatal)
- Ketoacidosis
- Diet
- Drugs (insulins, oral hypoglycaemic agents and pregnancy)

Other endocrinopathies:
- Thyroid (diagnosis, assessment, antibodies, therapy, fetal hazards)
- Adrenal (Addison's disease, acute adrenal failure, congenital adrenal hyperplasia, phaeochromocytoma)
- Pituitary (prolactinoma, hypopituitarism, diabetes insipidus)

Infectious diseases:
- Investigation of pyrexia
- Serological tests
- Principles (prevention, detection, isolation)
- Therapy (prophylaxis, immunization, antibiotics, antiviral agents)
- Maternal (preterm prelabour rupture of membranes, preterm labour, chorioamnionitis, puerperal sepsis, mastitis, urinary tract infection, wound infections, septic shock, malaria, other tropical infections and infestations)
- Fetus and neonate (streptococcus, gonococcus, syphilis, toxoplasma, listeria, haemophilus, chlamydia, mycoplasma, ureaplasma, herpes hominis, rubella, cytomegalovirus, varicella, hepatitis A, hepatitis B, hepatitis C, parvovirus, influenza, human immunodeficiency virus, neonatal sepsis)

Maternal complications due to pregnancy:
- Antepartum haemorrhage
- Amniotic fluid embolism
- Sheehan syndrome

Figure 1.3. Appendix to Curriculum Module 9: Maternal Medicine. Details of knowledge criteria

the (unpublished) Part 1 MRCOG Working Group's Report to the RCOG Council (December 2005) is pertinent here:

'Even a cursory look at developments in obstetrics and gynae-cology over the last 30 years – the length of time over which we expect colleagues to practise – demonstrates the extent to which the technological revolution has already changed our specialty. Ultrasound, laparoscopy, IVF, fetal blood sampling and prenatal diagnosis are now all used in day-to-day clinical practice. None was in widespread use when our senior colleagues were newly appointed consultants. Molecular biology and genetics now have clinical applications in prenatal diagnosis, gynaecological oncol-ogy and reproductive medicine, and advances in gene therapy and stem cell science will undoubtedly be translated into practice in the next decade. Clinical epidemiology and statistics, and understanding of clinical risk, are other relatively new concepts that are deeply embedded within clinical practice.'

The summative Parts 1 and 2 MRCOG examinations are particularly suited to testing factual knowledge and also certain problem-solving skills using clinical evaluation and critical judgement. However, the examinations represent only two elements of the panoply of assess-ment processes employed during the 7 years of the training programme illustrated above. It is clear that not all the knowledge, skills, attitudes and competencies of the Curriculum can be assessed by traditional examinations. Although, for example, it may be possible to include a labour ward prioritisation station in the Part 2 MRCOG oral assess-ment, skills such as the willingness to consult and to work as part of a team are more appropriately tested by workplace-based assessments such as multi-source (360-degree) feedback. The Curriculum therefore comprises a variety of assessment tools, which are appropriate for different skills. Some skills may, however, be appropriately tested by more than one tool and on more than one occasion: for example, the skills of counselling and history taking may be assessed both in the Part 2 oral assessment and also in the workplace.

The concept of syllabus

It must be clear to the examination candidate exactly which subjects will be tested by the examination and which will be assessed by other means. For this reason, the College has produced a new syllabus for Parts 1 and 2 of the MRCOG examination (Appendices 1, 2 and 3). A syllabus may be defined as 'a document with an outline of all topics to be covered in a

MODULE 9 TOPIC: Maternal medicine

Competence Level: ☐ Basic Training | ☐ Intermediate Training | ▨ Advanced Training | ■ Not required

Skill	Observation		Direct Supervision		Independent Practice	
	Date	Signature of trainer	Date	Signature of trainer	Date	Signature of trainer
Diagnose, investigate and manage with appropriate consultation:						
Chronic hypertension						
Pre eclampsia with HELP						
Pre eclampsia with renal failure						
Pre eclampsia with severe liver disease						
Pre eclampsia with pulmonary oedema						
Pre eclampsia with eclampsia						
Renal disease – Hydronephrosis						
Renal disease – Reflux nephropathy						
Renal disease – Renal transplantation						
Acute renal failure (not PET)						
Cardiac disease – congenital heart disease						
Cardiac disease – Rheumatic heart disease						
Cardiac disease – Ischaemic heart disease						
Cardiac disease – Artificial heart valve						
Cardiac disease – Arrhythmia						
Cardiac disease – Perpartum cardiomyopathy						

Figure 1.4. Maternal Medicine: excerpt from Logbook

course to ensure consistency across institutions or tests.' A syllabus lists the topics to be learned to cover the curriculum and it provides trainees with a concise document in the public domain describing the subjects to be formally examined. Not all aspects of the curriculum are suitable for inclusion in the MRCOG syllabus. In the Part 2 MRCOG syllabus, for example, it is evident that Modules 4 and 19 are not relevant to the examination and that they will be assessed by other means.

The principal advantage of a syllabus is that it is an explicit and transparent reference list for both trainees and examiners. Most importantly, it ensures that the salient areas of the curriculum are not neglected. This, in turn, facilitates the blueprinting process for those in charge of setting the different components and papers of the examination. Blueprinting is a process applied to the both the Part 1 and Part 2 MRCOG examination to ensure that each examination diet contains an appropriate coverage of the most important topics of the syllabus and to avoid duplication in the various components of each examination. For further information on blueprinting, see Chapter 7. For this reason, since each examination diet is blueprinted separately, it is not permissible for candidates who are successful in the Part 2 MRCOG written papers to sit an oral assessment of a different examination diet, to which a different blueprint will apply.

The perennial problem with a syllabus lies in its adequate description of the level or depth of knowledge that is required for each subject. This problem is not unique to medicine. For example, a question might appear in an 'A' Level History examination concerning the causes of the First World War. A similar question might appear in a Degree-level examination, although the difference in coverage and depth between the two expected answers will be substantial. However, a careful reading of the relevant curriculum in conjunction with the associated syllabus should reveal the level of knowledge to be examined.

Part 1 MRCOG syllabus

The aim of the Part 1 MRCOG examination is to guide candidates to learn the important aspects of biological science that are relevant to the clinical practice of obstetrics and gynaecology. For a much fuller account of Part 1, see Chapter 2. Currently, the examination consists of multiple-choice questions (MCQs) and extended matching questions (EMQs), certain topics being more appropriately examined in one format rather than the other. Trainees are required pass the Part 1 MRCOG examination by the end of Basic Training (ST2), the examination being a prerequisite for entry to Intermediate Training (ST3).

The new syllabus for Part 1 MRCOG consists of two complementary parts: a written summary of the topics to be assessed and a matrix showing the same material in a diagrammatic, more visually accessible format (see Appendix 2 at the back of the book).

The rows of the matrix comprise the nineteen modules of the Curriculum, minus those already mentioned as not being examined by the MRCOG. The columns are grouped beneath four major thematic headings, beginning with the smallest, most basic unit (the cell); in turn, under these headings, are grouped the scientific disciplines to be examined, as follows:

Understanding cell function
Physiology
Endocrinology
Biochemistry

Understanding human structure
Anatomy
Embryology
Genetics

Understanding measurement and manipulation
Biophysics
Epidemiology/statistics
Pharmacology

Understanding illness
Immunology
Microbiology
Pathology

The intersection of each module and scientific discipline provides the examination candidate with more specific information on the topic to be examined. For example, at the intersection of Module 8, Antenatal care, and the subject Endocrinology lies the topic to be assessed: 'Endocrinology of pregnancy. The placenta as an endocrine gland.' At the intersection of Antenatal care and Anatomy we find 'Anatomical adaptations to pregnancy'. Of course, not all the scientific subjects are relevant to each module and blank squares will therefore appear in these instances. For example, there is clearly no entry at the intersection of the module Postoperative care and the subject of Embryology.

The value of the matrix is as a visual summary of the syllabus. The matrix is particularly useful as an overview of both the Curriculum and

MODULE 8: ANTENATAL CARE

You need knowledge of the maternal anatomical adaptations occurring in pregnancy, together with the endocrine and cellular physiology of the major organ systems in both the pregnant and nonpregnant state. You must understand the process of the graft-versus-host reaction and immunological adaptations occurring in pregnancy, as well as the underlying immunological processes of infection, anaphylactic and allergy reactions and the effects of immunosuppressive drugs. You need to understand viral biology, infection and infection screening in pregnancy. You also need an understanding of the pathology of lung, renal and cardiac systems, the common haemoglobinopathies and connective tissue disorders. You should be able to define and interpret data on maternal mortality.

You need to understand the development and function of the placenta in pregnancy, with a specific knowledge of how the placenta handles drugs.

You should understand the principles of inheritance, the features and effects of common inherited disorders. You need a knowledge of normal fetal physiology and development, together with the aetiology of fetal malformations and growth problems. You should be able to define and interpret data on neonatal and perinatal mortality.

Figure 1.5. Prose version of Module 8 of the Part 1 MRCOG Syllabus

the Part 1 MRCOG syllabus and also as an aid to examination revision. A differently formatted version of the syllabus – the same information in continuous prose – is also available. For example, the syllabus entry for Module 8 is shown in Figure 1.5.

It is immediately obvious that the matrix and the syllabus are complementary aids; the availability of the same information in two mutually reinforcing formats is intended to be maximally helpful to the examination candidate. Moreover, the syllabus is deliberately written in a personal style, which addresses the candidate directly; for example: 'You need knowledge of...', 'You need to understand...', and 'You should be able to define and understand...'

ANATOMY

Comprehensive knowledge of the regional anatomy of the pelvis, abdomen, thorax, breast, thigh, endocrine glands, hypothalamus, spinothalamic tracts and meninges. Detailed knowledge of relevant bones, joints, muscles, blood vessels, lymphatics, nerve supply and histology. Basic understanding of cell structure.

PHYSIOLOGY

Comprehensive knowledge of human physiology with particular reference to the male and female reproductive systems, pregnancy, the fetus and the neonate. Quantitative information about common physiological activities. Understanding of the principles of nutrition, water, electrolyte and acid base balance and cell biology.

Figure 1.6. An example of the syllabus from the 'old' Part 1 examination

A comparison between the new dual-format syllabus for Part 1 MRCOG and the old syllabus is particularly striking. The old syllabus had the major disadvantage of not being explicitly derived from a published curriculum. It was also far less detailed, as illustrated by the example shown in Figure 1.6, which is a simple listing, enjoining the examination candidate, somewhat unhelpfully, to know all there is to know about the contents of the list.

Part 2 MRCOG syllabus

The Part 2 MRCOG examination consists of a written component (MCQ, EMQ and SAQs) followed by an oral assessment for those candidates who are successful in the written papers. The Part 2 MRCOG syllabus does not have a matrix but, like the Part 1 syllabus, it follows the modules of the Curriculum with entries in continuous prose addressing the reader directly in the second person. For example, the syllabus entry for Module14 is shown in Figure 1.7.

As with Part 1, the syllabus for Part 2 MRCOG is the candidate's principal guide to the topics to be examined in the Part 2 examination. Since the syllabus is derived directly from the curriculum, it is designed to be read in the context of, and with reference to, the entire curriculum. Candidates must pass the Part 2 MRCOG examination by the end of Intermediate Training (ST5) and it is therefore a prerequisite for entry to Advanced Training (ST6) and to increasingly independent practice.

MODULE 14: SUBFERTILITY

The examiners will expect you to demonstrate appropriate knowledge, skills and attitudes in relation to subfertility. This includes an understanding of the epidemiology, aetiology, pathogenesis, clinical treatment and prognosis of all aspects of male and female fertility problems. Your knowledge will include indications, limitations and interpretation of relative investigations and treatments in relation to both male and female including disorders of development and endometriosis. You will be expected to have a broad-based knowledge of assisted reproductive techniques including: ovulation induction, in vitro fertilisation and intracytoplasmic sperm injection, gamete donation, surrogacy and the legal and ethical implications of these procedures.

Figure 1.7. Entry for Module 14 of the Part 2 MRCOG Syllabus

Again, as with Part 1, a comparison with the old Part 2 syllabus is instructive, as illustrated by the example shown in Figure 1.8, taken from the old syllabus. It is immediately obvious that the old entry for Infertility is much less detailed and less helpful than that for the new syllabus entry for Module 14 (Figure 1.7).

Conclusion

With the advent of the College's new Curriculum and Syllabus for the Part 1 and Part 2 MRCOG examinations, candidates for these examinations have never before been better informed or supported. In the past, candidates preparing for the Membership examinations had a dearth of formal guidance from the College to assist them. There was no formal curriculum that could be referred to, and the examination syllabuses were 'minimalist' as the extracts cited above demonstrate.

INFERTILITY

Causes, investigation and management of infertility together with basic knowledge in the techniques involved in *in vitro* fertilisation.

Figure 1.8. Example from the 'old' Part 2 MRCOG Syllabus

PMETB requires that the format and design of College assessment systems and their methods should be appropriate to what is being tested, such as:[4]

(a)   clinical skills

(b)   knowledge and decision-making

(c)   interpersonal (communication) skills

(d)   competence in particular areas.

As we have noted, not all of the above will be appropriately tested in the MRCOG examinations. The MRCOG examinations are particularly useful for the testing of knowledge, clinical problem-solving skills, as well as attitudes and communication in the Part 2 oral assessment. The precise scope of the MRCOG examinations is clearly defined by both the Curriculum and by the Syllabus for Parts 1 and 2 to enable candidates to tailor their preparation and revision for these examinations in a focused and targeted manner.

The new Curriculum developed by the RCOG has clear learning outcomes, which make plain the precise knowledge, skills, attitudes and behaviours that specialist doctors in training must attain. It is intended that these learning outcomes should not be set in stone but rather that they should be updated in line with developing research and evidence and, as medical practice changes, should also take account of patients' expectations. Any such changes will be immediately reflected in the examination syllabuses and announced to examination candidates via the College's website.

References

1.   Postgraduate Medical Education and Training Board. What is Curriculum? [www.pmetb.org.uk/fileadmin/user/Communications/Publications/PMETB_what_is_curriculum.pdf].
2.   Postgraduate Medical Education and Training Board. Standards for Curriculum Development: Background Paper. September 2004 [www.pmetb.org.uk/fileadmin/user/Communications/Publications/PMETB_background_paper_-_standards_for_curriculum_development__September_2004_.pdf].
3.   Postgraduate Medical Education and Training Board. Standards for Curricula. Revised March 2005 [www.pmetb.org.uk/fileadmin/user/Communications/Publications/PMETB_standards_for_curricula__March_2005_.pdf].
4.   Postgraduate Medical Education and Training Board. Principles of Good Medical Education and Training. 2005 [www.pmetb.org.uk/media/pdf/o/b/PMETB-GMC_Principles_of_good_medical_education_and_training_(2005).pdf].

2 The Part 1 MRCOG examination

Introduction

The new Specialty Training Curriculum covers basic, intermediate and advanced training in obstetrics and gynaecology, with the Part 1 MRCOG syllabus forming an important foundation of the overall template for core training in the specialty. The Part 1 MRCOG examination represents an important summative assessment of the applied clinical sciences; that is, basic sciences as relevant to the clinical practice of obstetrics and gynaecology.

The Part 1 MRCOG examination has recently been modernised following the recommendations of the (unpublished) Part 1 MRCOG Working Group Report to Council in December 2005.

The report noted that the pass rate for the Part 1 examination had been declining over the last decade, partly reflecting a reduction in the teaching of basic science at undergraduate level.

As part of the modernisation process, a new Part 1 syllabus has been defined with applied clinical science knowledge mapped against modules of the core training curriculum. The Part 1 question bank has been reviewed, updated and added to with a view to increasing the clinical relevance of the basic science questions. A decision was made to include extended matching questions (EMQs) alongside traditional multiple-choice questions (MCQs) from September 2007 onwards.

This chapter focuses on the changes to the Part 1 MRCOG examination, particularly the new format EMQs, with hints on how to approach the new-style questions.

Background

The Part 1 MRCOG Working Group was set up during 2005 to ensure that the Part 1 examination remained 'fit for purpose' and to make recommendations concerning the syllabus, content and format of a reformed examination. The group was required to:

- define the core knowledge and competencies required of Part 1 MRCOG candidates as a prerequisite for progressing to the Part 2 examination
- review the new core curriculum in obstetrics and gynaecology with particular reference to the appropriateness of the clinical sciences component for Part 1 candidates
- devise a new syllabus for the Part 1 MRCOG examination; and to review and update the Part 1 question bank.

The Part 1 MRCOG comprises a clinical sciences examination set in the context of rapid advances in bioscience where investigations and treatments derived from the 'new' bioscience of the 1980s and 1990s are now impacting upon clinical practice. Clinicians are required to incorporate these tools into their clinical work and to advise patients of their utility. Similarly, clinicians need to be able to engage with scientific innovations, to understand the opportunities and limitations of new technology and to be confident when appraising new technologies. This requires an adequate grounding in clinical science. Examples of new bioscience being used in everyday practice include ultrasound, laparoscopy, in vitro fertilisation, fetal blood sampling and prenatal diagnosis. Molecular biology and genetics have clinical applications in prenatal diagnosis, gynaecological oncology and reproductive medicine, and advances in gene therapy and stem cell science will undoubtedly be translated into practice in the next decade. Clinical epidemiology, statistics and an understanding of clinical risk are other relatively new concepts that are becoming increasingly deeply embedded within clinical practice. In contrast, some subjects essential to the trainee are unchanging, such as embryology and the surgical anatomy of the pelvis.

Since knowledge continues to be the single best determinant of expertise in a subject, it remains essential that a trainee understands, assimilates and retains knowledge of the basic clinical sciences. One of the aims of the Part 1 MRCOG examination is, therefore, to help to drive the learning of important aspects of biological science as relevant to the clinical practice of obstetrics and gynaecology.

While there have been rapid advances in bioscience over recent years, the teaching of clinical science in UK medical schools has seen a trend towards integration into clinical curricula, with a move towards more teaching being undertaken by clinical staff and an overall reduction in basic science content. In addition, the move towards problem-based learning has probably contributed towards a reduction in basic science teaching in favour of a more 'applied' knowledge base. The reduction in basic science being taught at undergraduate level means that Part 1 MRCOG candidates are facing the examination needing to learn rather than to revise basic clinical sciences. Partly as a result of these trends, the last few years have seen a reduction in the number of candidates passing the Part 1 MRCOG examination.

The Part 1 MRCOG Working Group recommendations included improving the clinical relevance of the question bank, an alteration in the distribution of questions across subjects, the inclusion of EMQs alongside MCQs and changes to standard setting when determining the pass mark for each examination.

Implementation of the new Part 1 MRCOG examination

As a result of selecting more clinically relevant questions from the existing Part 1 question bank, pass rates improved in 2006 to 36.8 % overall and to 42.2% for UK and Republic of Ireland graduates.

A new Part 1 MRCOG syllabus has been defined, with applied clinical science knowledge mapped against modules of the core training curriculum, details of which are available on the RCOG website[1,2] in both text and matrix formats, and shown in Appendices 1 and 2 to this volume. This mapping allows blueprinting of the examination to ensure that major aspects of the curriculum are covered at each examination.

The distribution of questions within the Part 1 examination has been revised and incorporated into the examination papers. It was recognised that new questions were required to reflect the new curriculum and EMQs have been included alongside the traditional MCQs from September 2007.[3] Figures 2.1 and 2.2 show the distribution of question topics, although naturally this will vary somewhat from sitting to sitting. The figures also indicate new question areas being included in future Part 1 MRCOG examinations, such as clinical trial design and analysis, molecular biology and genomics.

EXTENDED MATCHING QUESTIONS

EMQs have been introduced into the Part 1 examination for the following reasons:

- They increase the validity and reliability of the examination.
- EMQs test more complex understanding than MCQs and reduce the inherent 'cues' of MCQ formats.
- EMQ questions allow relationships between facts to be tested.

- They allow questions to be constructed that are more relevant to clinical practice.
- They are computer marked ensuring complete accuracy.

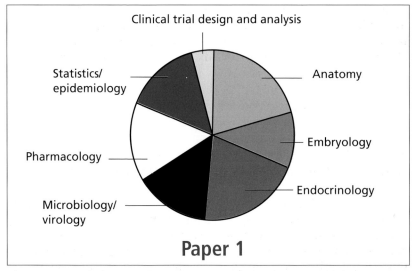

Figure 2.1. Distribution of question topics within Paper 1 of the Part 1 examination

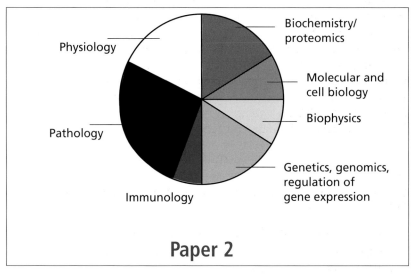

Figure 2.2. Distribution of question topics within Paper 2 of the Part 2 examination

A recent literature review on question formats in medical examinations concluded that 'there is a wealth of evidence that EMQs are the fairest format'.[4] They are now widely and profitably used in undergraduate-level medical examinations and are increasingly being incorporated into postgraduate examinations. Internal trials were held at the RCOG and EMQs were introduced into the Part 2 MRCOG examination in September 2006. At the time of writing, the Part 2 EMQs have been run at three 'real' Part 2 MRCOG diets and the early data suggest that the format performs very well, with EMQs proving to be excellent discriminators. Candidates performing well overall in the Part 2 written examination generally achieved high marks on the EMQ paper and candidates performing poorly overall received low marks.

In recognition of their increased length and complexity, in particular with regard to the extra time required to read them, EMQs have been assigned a longer time for completion than MCQs.[5] Each 'item' or question within an EMQ will be worth three marks compared with one mark for each twig of an MCQ (each MCQ 'stem' consists of five 'twigs').

EMQ question format

Each EMQ question consists of an 'option' or answer list (lettered to reflect the answer sheet), a lead-in statement (which sets the question into context and tells the candidate what to do) and then a list of one to three questions or 'items' (each numbered to match the answer sheet). The best way to understand this format is to look at and work through the examples provided in the Appendix at the end of this chapter. The option lists will often be in alphabetical or numerical order for ease of reference.

A standardised blank template is used in the construction of EMQs (Figure 2.3). For comparison, a blank MCQ template is shown in Figure 2.4.

Hints on answering EMQs

In addition to ensuring that they have the necessary knowledge, candidates are advised to be aware of the different question formats before entering the Part 1 MRCOG examination and to have practised answering questions in these formats. EMQs can be written with a single list of 'options' or answers or they may be combined into a table format, thereby increasing the number of elements of the syllabus examined by a single item, as well as assessing a candidate's ability to link knowledge.

The answer sheet for the new Part 1 papers will be similar to those used for the MCQ papers.

Although the answer sheet will provide 20 possible answers, the option lists for questions may not use all of these. Most option lists will

Author	
Curriculum module link (number and title)	
Subject area and theme	
Domain (e.g. anatomy, pharmacology)	

OPTIONS

A		K	
B		L	
C		M	
D		N	
E		O	
F		P	
G		Q	
H		R	
I		S	
J		T	

INSTRUCTIONS

For each...described below, choose the **single** most...from the above list of options. Each option may be used once, more than once or not at all.

Item 1	
Answer (please include option letter and full answer)	

Item 2	
Answer (please include option letter and full answer)	

Item 3	
Answer (please include option letter and full answer)	

Figure 2.3. Standardised template for constructing EMQs

Author	
Curriculum module link (number and title)	
Subject area and theme	
Domain (e.g. anatomy, pharmacology)	

Stem:		Answer (T/F):
Item 1:		
Item 2:		
Item 3:		
Item 4:		
Item 5:		

Figure 2.4. Standardised template for constructing MCQs

provide 10–14 answer options. The option lists will nearly always be in alphabetical or numerical order for ease of reference; if not, they will be in the most appropriate order for quick reference.

The most important element of the format is that you must select the single answer that fits best. You may think that there are several possible answers but you must choose only the most likely from the option list. As with the MCQ paper, if two or more boxes are marked on the same question, no mark will be awarded, even if one of the answers chosen is the correct one. It is therefore important to ensure that any mistakes are clearly and fully erased.

EMQs are designed to be fair and unambiguous. The following points should be remembered when answering them:

- The questions have been carefully constructed.
- Read and follow the instructions given in the stem.
- Read the instructions, questions or 'items' before reading the 'option' or answer list.
- **There is only one correct answer.**
- Beware of distractors within the list of options or answers.
- Options or answers may be used once, more than once, or not at all.

Examples of EMQs are provided on the RCOG website and in various other sources.[5-7] Neither the MCQs nor EMQs are negatively marked.

Initially, EMQs will form approximately 20% of the overall Part 1 examination, with 20 'items' or questions relating to approximately six lists of options in each paper. The papers currently comprise the distribution of questions shown in Figure 2.5.

If the EMQs perform as well as expected, it is likely that this percentage will gradually increase in the future. If this change occurs, candidates will be given plenty of advance notice.

Marking of EMQs

The current value of each correct MCQ answer remains the same. Each correct EMQ answer will be worth the equivalent of three correct MCQ answers. The timetable for the two Part 1 MRCOG examination papers will remain the same two papers of 2 hours each, separated by a lunch break. Candidates' time management will be important and it is recommended that candidates spend approximately 96 minutes on the MCQs and 24 minutes on the EMQs.

KEY POINTS FOR EMQS

- Knowledge is the single best determinant of expertise in a subject so thorough preparation for the examination is of the utmost importance.

- It is important to understand the relationship between different facts when studying the scientific foundations of obstetrics and gynaecology; that is, the application of basic clinical sciences to clinical practice.

- EMQs are useful in testing the understanding of a subject.

- EMQs complement the high reliability of the MCQ format in the Part 1 MRCOG examination while enhancing validity.

- Good preparation and familiarity with the EMQ and MCQ formats are key to passing examinations.

MULTIPLE CHOICE QUESTIONS

The tried and tested true/false multiple-choice format continues to have a very strong role in the Part 1 examination. Indeed, while the proportion of MCQs may in time diminish to make way for more EMQs, it is highly unlikely that they will disappear from the examination com-

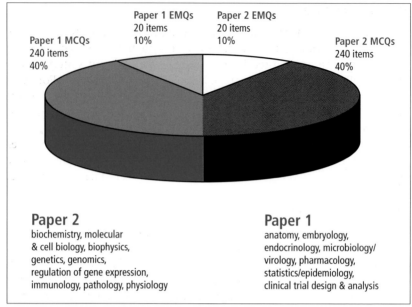

Paper 1 EMQs
20 items
10%

Paper 2 EMQs
20 items
10%

Paper 1 MCQs
240 items
40%

Paper 2 MCQs
240 items
40%

Paper 2
biochemistry, molecular
& cell biology, biophysics,
genetics, genomics,
regulation of gene expression,
immunology, pathology, physiology

Paper 1
anatomy, embryology,
endocrinology, microbiology/
virology, pharmacology,
statistics/epidemiology,
clinical trial design & analysis

Figure 2.5. Distribution of questions within the new Part 1 examination

pletely. MCQs are highly competent at testing a large and diverse amount
of information, such as the Part 1 MRCOG syllabus, in a relatively short
period of time. They make efficient use of testing time and have high
content validity. To maintain reliability, reproducibility and validity
without using the MCQ format, examinations would generally have to
be considerably longer. Careful question writing diminishes some of the
pitfalls of the format, such as overly cueing 'test-wise' candidates, and the
MRCOG MCQ question bank is carefully constructed and under
continual scrutiny, review and revision.

While they cannot test integration of knowledge in the manner of
EMQs, MCQs can test knowledge in a straightforward manner. They
generally elicit either a clear 'know' or 'don't know'. As ever, good, varied
reading and revision are the key to success. A secure knowledge base is
essential for performing well at this question format.

Candidates usually have extensive experience of the MCQ format
from their undergraduate assessments but, since they form such a substantial part of the Part 1 examination, it is worth bearing in mind some
points peculiar to the format while revising. Plenty of practice, a good
proportion under simulated examination conditions, is therefore
recommended.

MCQ question format

The format, particularly when compared with that of EMQs, is a simple one. Each question (numbers 21 to 68 on each of the two question papers) has a 'stem' printed in bold and five component statements or 'twigs', following on, which are labelled A, B, C, D and E. For each statement, the candidate must decide whether it is true or false (correct or incorrect) and must mark it accordingly on their answer sheet. A blank MCQ template is shown in Figure 2.4.

The examiners try to avoid phrasing questions as double negatives but on occasion this is impossible. Reading the question again slowly and carefully in such cases should help you to overcome this obstacle.

Hints on answering MCQs

Using the pencil provided, answer directly onto the answer sheet - this saves time and avoids transcription errors. Erase mistakes fully, as the scanner used for marking will not allocate a mark if it appears that both the true and false boxes are completed. Work systematically through the questions and answer those you know immediately at a good pace, then attempt the questions you found difficult. This should allow you to build up additional time.

Do not go back over the questions already answered, unless there is a specific piece of information that you have remembered since you answered it. Your first answer is almost always the correct one. The questions range from easy to hard. Do not be anxious if the answer appears obvious – you are probably correct. As ever, read the questions carefully. Small points of language or fact can completely change the answer. Trick questions, however, are not used. Examiners do not aim to trick you, so, if a question appears 'tricky', read it again slowly and carefully to check that you have understood the meaning properly.

Approximately 10% of the MCQ questions in Part 1 MRCOG will be 'test questions'. These will not contribute to your final mark but are being assessed for possible future inclusion in the question bank. Hence if you come across a question which is oddly worded or is unusual in some way, this may well be a 'test' question which still contains some flaws. It is obviously vital to answer all questions on the assumption that they carry marks and not to try to 'second guess' the examiners.

Marking of MCQs

Just as for the EMQs, there is **no** negative marking. It is thus vitally important to complete your answer sheet fully. Even complete guesses will after all have a 50% chance of being correct, and wrong answers are not penalised. Educated guesswork applied to the question may well increase this 50:50 chance substantially and it is therefore recommended.

Specimen MCQ questions

1. **Concerning the abdominal vasculature:**
   A. The superior rectal artery arises from the inferior mesenteric artery.
   B. The right gastric artery arises from the hepatic artery.
   C. The right gastro-epiploic artery arises from the splenic artery.
   D. The left gastro-epiploic artery arises from the gastroduodenal artery.
   E. The inferior pancreaticoduodenal artery arises from the superior mesenteric artery.

2. **The pudendal nerve**
   A. derives its fibres from the second, third and fourth sacral segments.
   B. runs between the pyriformis and coccygeus muscles before leaving the pelvis.
   C. has the pudendal artery on its medial side as it lies of the ischial spine.
   D. gives off the inferior haemorrhoidal (rectal) nerve in the pudendal canal.
   E. innervates the clitoris.

3. **The effectiveness of a combined oral contraceptive pill may be reduced by:**
   A. bromocriptine.
   B. phenytoin.
   C. rifampicin.
   D. ampicillin.
   E. sodium valproate.

4. **The following are Gram negative bacteria:**
   A. *Streptococcus pneumoniae.*
   B. *Haemophilus influenzae.*
   C. *Neisseria meningitides.*
   D. *Clostridium perfringens.*
   E. *Listeria monocytogenes.*

5. **The menarche**
   A. usually follows an ovulatory cycle.
   B. is preceded by the thelarche.
   C. occurs earlier in girls below normal weight.
   D. is preceded by the adrenarche.
   E. is followed by the growth spurt.

6. **Epitheloid granulomata are characteristics of**
   A. Crohn's disease.
   B. typhoid fever.
   C. sarcoidosis.
   D. Hodgkin's disease.
   E. leprosy.

Specimen MCQ questions – answer key

1. A. True
   B. True
   C. False
   D. False
   E. False

2. A. True
   B. True
   C. False
   D. True
   E. True

3. A. False
   B. True
   C. True
   D. True
   E. False

4. A. False
   B. True
   C. True
   D. False
   E. False

5. A. False
   B. True
   C. False
   D. True
   E. False

6. A. True
   B. False
   C. True
   D. False
   E. True

Blueprinting

Blueprinting ensures the even coverage of both the subjects and domains of the curriculum and syllabus and also ensures that the examination is neither too predictable nor unpredictable. Blueprinting confirms that subject areas comprising core knowledge for the specialty are suitably covered to test trainees comprehensively.[8] The new MRCOG Core Curriculum allows examinations to be blueprinted and maps the Part 1 MRCOG as a component part of the overall process of assessment for future consultants in the specialty. Part 1 and Part 2 MRCOG form a single integrated and blueprinted examination of relevant factual knowledge and clinical skills in the specialty, ensuring appropriately weighted domain and subject coverage. See Chapter 7 for more information on blueprinting.

Standard setting

Standard setting, to determine the pass mark, is already undertaken for the Part 1 MRCOG examination.[9] The aim of standard setting is to improve the fairness and validity of the examination and to set levels of competence required for success in the examination. Standard setting produces a correct criterion-referenced pass mark by assessing the difficulty of individual papers, using a modified Angoff method. This allows proactive adjustment of question difficulty to ensure that papers are neither too hard nor too easy overall for candidates.[8] See Chapter 7 for more information about standard setting.

References

1. Royal College of Obstetricians and Gynaecologists. Part One and Curriculum Matrix. 2007 [www.rcog.org.uk/index.asp?PageID=1912].
2. Royal College of Obstetricians and Gynaecologists. Part 1 MRCOG syllabus summary. 2007 [www.rcog.org.uk/index.asp?PageID=174].
3. Royal College of Obstetricians and Gynaecologists. Format for the Part 1 MRCOG Examination. 2007 [www.rcog.org.uk/index.asp?PageID=1862].
4. McCoubrie P. Improving the fairness of multiple-choice questions: a literature review. *Medical Teacher* 2004;26(8):709–12.
5. Duthie S, Fiander A, Hodges P. Extended matched questions: a new component of the part 1 examination leading to membership of the Royal College of Obstetricians and Gynaecologists. *The Obstetrician & Gynaecologist* 2007;9:189–94.
6. Duthie J, Hodges P. EMQs for the MRCOG Part 1. London: RCOG Press; 2007.
7. Thilaganathan B, Fiander AN, editors. *MRCOG Part 1 Essential Revision: a complete guide to the new-style examination*. London: RCOG Press; 2008.
8. Hodges P. Blueprinting the RCOG examinations. *The Obstetrician & Gynaecologist* 2007;9:53–7.
9. Royal College of Obstetricians and Gynaecologists. Standard Setting. 2007 [www.rcog.org.uk/index.asp?PageID=176].

Appendix
Examples of Part 1 MRCOG EMQs

Example 1

Curriculum module	**9 Maternal Medicine**
Subject	**Maternal infections: micro-organism types and transplacental infection risks**
Domain	**Microbiology**

OPTIONS

	Maternal disease	Type of micro-organism	Risk of transplacental infection
A	Babesiosis	Protozoan	No
B	Babesiosis	Protozoan	Yes
C	Coccidioidomycosis	Fungus	No
D	Coccidioidomycosis	Fungus	Yes
E	Malaria	Bacterium	Yes
F	Malaria	Protozoan	No
G	Malaria	Protozoan	Yes
H	Malaria	Virus	Yes
I	Q fever	Rickettsia	Yes
J	Q fever	Virus	Yes
K	Schistosomiasis	Helminth	Yes
L	Schistosomiasis	Protozoan	Yes
M	Syphilis	Protozoan	Yes
N	Syphilis	Spirochete	No
O	Syphilis	Spirochete	Yes
P	Syphilis	Virus	Yes

Q	Tuberculosis	Bacterium	No
R	Tuberculosis	Bacterium	Yes
S	Tuberculosis	Fungus	No
T	Tuberculosis	Protozoan	No

INSTRUCTIONS

The options above refer to different maternal diseases, which are caused by micro-organisms, the type of organism and whether or not there is a risk of transplacental infection. Select the single correct profile for each of the micro-organisms in the items below. Each option may be used once, more than once or not at all.

Item 1:   *Treponema pallidum*
Answer: O – Syphilis; Spirochete; Yes

Item 2:   *Mycobacterium tuberculosis*
Answer: R – Tuberculosis; Bacterium; Yes

Item 3:   Plasmodium falciparum
Answer: G – Malaria; Protozoan; Yes

Note on example

This EMQ has 20 options, a clear lead-in statement and three items. The lead-in statement explains to the candidate that the list of options refers to different maternal diseases that are caused by micro-organisms. The second column in the list of options states different types of microbes and the third column indicates whether or not there is a risk of transplacental infection. The examination candidate is asked to select the correct profile from the list of options for each of the questions in the worked example. Using this format, the examination verifies that the candidate understands that:

- *Treponema pallidum* is the cause of syphilis
- *Treponema pallidum* is a spirochete
- There is a risk of transplacental infection.

There are many other facts that are also relevant including mode of transmission, clinical features (typical and atypical), epidemiology, diagnosis and sensitivity to penicillin. These can be incorporated into the test profile.

Equally, the profile connecting different facts about another organism is tested in Item 2. The candidate must avoid the distractors that are present and select the option that describes *Mycobacterium tuberculosis* as:

- the cause of tuberculosis
- a bacterium
- capable of transplacental infection.

A similar profile is tested for *Plasmodium falciparum* in Item 3.

Example 2

Module	**17 Gynaecological Oncology**
Subject	**Tumour susceptibility**
Domain	**Genetics**

OPTIONS

A   Adrenocortical cancer and melanoma

B   Brain tumours, sarcoma of bone and soft tissue

C   Breast cancer and ovarian cancer

D   Breast cancer and retinoblastoma

E   Breast cancer, brain tumours, adrenocortical cancer, leukaemia, sarcoma of bone and soft tissue

F   Breast cancer, brain tumours, endometrial cancer

G   Breast cancer, ovarian cancer, adrenocortical cancer, acute myeloid leukaemia

H   Cancer of the rectum and cancer of the stomach

I   Cancer of the rectum, cancer of the endometrium, cancer of the stomach and cancer of the bile duct

J   Colonic cancer and cancer of the stomach

K   Colorectal cancer and bronchopulmonary cancer

L   Colorectal cancer, cancer of the endometrium, cancer of the stomach and cancer of the bile duct

M   Ovarian cancer

N   Ovarian cancer and retinoblastoma

O   Retinoblastoma

P   Retinoblastoma and adenocarcinoma of the cervix

Q   Retinoblastoma and adrenocortical cancer

R   Retinoblastoma and cancer of the bladder

S   Retinoblastoma and cancer of the endometrium

T   Retinoblastoma and osteosarcoma

INSTRUCTIONS

The list of options describes different malignant conditions. The items below refer to conditions that increase tumour susceptibility. Select the single option that indicates which tumour or tumours an individual would be at increased risk of acquiring for each of the conditions in the items below. Each option may be used once, more than once or not at all.

Item 1:   *BRCA1*
Answer: C – Breast cancer and ovarian cancer

Item 2:   *BRCA2*
Answer: C – Breast cancer and ovarian cancer

Item 3:   Hereditary retinoblastoma
Answer: T – Retinoblastoma and osteosarcoma

Notes on example

Functional distractors can be used in the list of options to distract the borderline or weak candidate who is not entirely sure of the answer. A functional distractor may be based on a 'real' condition or a hypothetical (imaginary) condition, as this example demonstrates. Item 1 asks about tumour susceptibility for *BRCA1* mutation; most candidates would know that breast cancer is a significant risk. However, five of the options (C to G) contain breast cancer. The candidate must be sure that option C is the correct answer. Retinoblastoma is a rare condition but hereditary retinoblastoma increases the relative risk of acquiring osteosarcoma by a factor of approximately 2000. Therefore, the answer to Item 3 is T. Again, there are several functional distractors for the candidate. Both the list of options and the items can be varied in future, as the scientific community in the field of tumour susceptibility acquires further knowledge.

Example 3

		Author	**Mr SJ Duthie**
		Theme	**Understanding human structure**
		Domain	**Anatomy of the pelvis**

OPTIONS

	Length	Mesentery	Arterial blood supply	Lymphatic drainage
A	40 cm	Yes	Inferior mesenteric artery	Pre-aortic and inferior mesenteric nodes
B	50 cm	Yes	Inferior mesenteric artery	Pre-aortic and inferior mesenteric nodes
C	12 cm	No	Superior mesenteric artery	Pre-aortic and inferior mesenteric nodes
D	47 cm	No	Superior mesenteric artery	Pre-aortic and superior mesenteric nodes
E	60 cm	No	Internal iliac artery	Pre-aortic and celiac nodes
F	12 cm	No	Inferior mesenteric artery	Internal iliac lymph nodes, pre-aortic and inferior mesenteric nodes
G	12 cm	Yes	Inferior mesenteric artery	Internal iliac lymph nodes, pre-aortic and inferior mesenteric nodes
H	20 cm	No	Inferior mesenteric artery	Internal iliac lymph nodes, pre-aortic and inferior mesenteric nodes
I	12 cm	Yes	Superior mesenteric artery	Internal iliac nodes
J	15 cm	No	Internal iliac artery	External iliac nodes

INSTRUCTIONS

The list of options describes a pelvic organ in terms of its length, whether or not it has a mesenteric attachment, its arterial blood supply and lymphatic drainage. Select the most appropriate profile for each of the organs in the items below. Each option may be used once, more than once or not at all.

Item 1:   Sigmoid colon
Answer: A; 40 cm; Yes; Inferior mesenteric artery; Pre-aortic and inferior mesenteric nodes

Item 2:   Rectum
Answer: F; 12 cm; No; Inferior mesenteric artery; Internal iliac lymph nodes, pre-aortic and inferior mesenteric nodes

3 Part 2 Multiple-choice question paper

Introduction

A multiple-choice question gives candidates the option of selecting an answer from a given list. There are several types of MCQs but the Part 2 MRCOG examination requires the candidate to choose between two options – 'True' or 'False'. Although the MCQ format inevitably encourages the weaker candidate to try to guess the correct answer, it introduces flexibility, in that examiners are able to assess candidates on important aspects of the curriculum that would be difficult to incorporate into the other components of the examination. The MCQ format allows a large range of knowledge to be tested quickly. EMQs are essentially a variation of MCQs and complement the 'True' and 'False' type of questions. The reliability of an examination depends to a large extent upon its reproducibility, and the MCQ paper has repeatedly been shown to be one of the most reproducible parts of the Part 2 MRCOG examination.

Advantages and disadvantages of MCQs

Some of the advantages of the MCQ paper are:

- It can be easily and reliably marked. Computer marking avoids any chance of human error and bias and also allows for a rapid turn-around time between receipt of the papers and release of the results.

- It can be set at different cognitive levels; for example, one that challenges the candidates' ability to recall facts, to apply factual knowledge to a given situation or to evaluate information. These levels are different and require different approaches to working out the answers to the questions.

- The questions can be set with a specific objective in mind; for example, to find out whether specific areas of a given topic have been covered by the candidates. The published curriculum and syllabus clearly define the various subjects and domains to be assessed, and the MCQ is an effective assessment tool for most of these.

- If the questions are designed properly, then candidates with poor reading skills or whose first language is not English will not be disadvantaged. However, for candidates with such problems the sheer number of questions means that the proportion of marks that could potentially be lost is small and therefore impacts minimally on the overall score. This contrasts with the short-answer questions, where the misreading of one question can result in a significant loss of marks.

- It is easy to obtain statistical information on each question, which allows examiners to assess whether a particular question performed well as a good discriminator or, alternatively, was inappropriate or poorly designed. Thus, the statistics obtained from the examination software allows questions to be ranked into different categories (such as difficult or easy) and their ability to discriminate between the poor and good candidates.

- Different aspects of the same questions may be used in different examinations, while assessing the same component of the curriculum.

- It enables broader aspects of the curriculum to be covered than would otherwise have been possible. Candidates are therefore forced to read as widely as possible rather than concentrating on possible topics for the examination.

The disadvantages of the MCQ paper include:

- It encourages guessing where knowledge is poor or lacking. With the 'True'/'False' type of questions, the candidate has a 50% chance of guessing the correct answer.

- Candidates are often cued with the answer by clues within the text of the question.

- Examiners tend to favour questions within their area of specialist knowledge, as they are easy to set.

- Creativity cannot easily be tested. However, this is tested by the discursive short-answer questions.

- Ambiguity is often difficult to eliminate completely; this makes setting the questions a lengthy process.

- MCQs cannot test the candidates' ability to express themselves or to develop an argument.

- There is always the temptation to use pre-existing questions rather than ensuring that the question exactly tests a particular area within the curriculum.

Preparing for the MCQ

The preparation required for this part of the examination is different from that required for either the short-answer question paper or the oral assessment. While it may be possible to second-guess which areas may be assessed in the SAQ paper and to plan revision accordingly, it is not possible to apply this principle to the MCQ paper, simply because of the number of questions in the paper and the fact that questions may be from any part of the curriculum.

The best way to prepare for the MCQ paper is therefore to read as broadly as possible. Every effort should be made to concentrate less on the memorising of facts and more on the understanding of basic principles and concepts. This will ensure that you are able to reason an answer rather than to guess. However, no single textbook can be recommended as being fully comprehensive. Candidates are encouraged to acquire at least one standard textbook in obstetrics and one in gynaecology. The best book is one that is sufficiently detailed (that is, it does not make assumptions about basic knowledge). In addition, it is highly recommended that candidates read most (if not all) the educational material produced by the RCOG. This will include the Green-top Guidelines, *BJOG* and *The Obstetrician & Gynaecologist* (TOG). Most review and risk management articles in TOG are accompanied by a series of MCQs and these provide an excellent opportunity for candidates not only to revise the topic but also to familiarise themselves with MCQs. Candidates are also advised regularly to check general medical journals such as the *BMJ*, *JAMA*, *New England Journal of Medicine* and *The Lancet*. These journals regularly publish not only seminal research, which often changes practice, but also review articles which provide excellent summaries of contemporary facts about the subject. You should also work through the tutorials provided within StratOG.net (www.stratog.net).

It is generally believed that assessment drives learning and it was for this reason that the RCOG published a series of past MCQ question papers (1997–2001).[1] This volume is one of the most useful revision tools for candidates. No candidate should sit the examination without having worked through the questions in the book. It is important to remember that, while the questions are taken directly from the RCOG bank of questions, some of them will have been updated as new information emerges. It is poor preparation simply to work from a copy to which answers have been supplied, as these may have been provided by another candidate who may not necessarily have got them right. Furthermore, such an approach might well provide the candidate with a false sense of security, as memory may take priority over understanding. Candidates should therefore work through not only the RCOG MCQ papers but also papers from courses and other textbooks.

How to approach the MCQ paper

The following general principles should provide guidance to candidates on how to approach the paper.

- Organise yourself and ensure that you understand the duration of the whole paper and the average time for each question. This will guarantee that you finish the paper.

- Read the question carefully before answering it. It is not uncommon to misread a question and therefore to answer it incorrectly. This is more likely to occur under examination conditions when you are stressed and nervous. For example, you may read, 'Which of the following features is associated with…' rather than 'Which of the following features is NOT associated with…' These types of mistake are further compounded when you see familiar questions. Always remember that examiners are constantly revising and updating questions and, although questions may appear familiar, they might have been changed. Ideally, you should treat each question in the paper as new.

- For most of the questions, the first impression is usually the correct one. Once you start agonising over the answer, you are more likely to get it wrong.

- Do not waste time over questions of which you are unsure; come back to them later. Another question in the paper may jog your memory and a few minutes sometimes may allow the subconscious to recall a vital 'pearl of wisdom'.

- Do not leave any question unanswered. Any educated guesses will increase your chances of getting it right by 50%. The MRCOG MCQ paper is not negatively marked so you will not lose marks for a wrong answer.

- Remember that common things occur commonly. If you come across a question on a topic about which you believe you are very knowledgeable but the content of the question is completely unfamiliar to you, then the chances are that you need to re-read the question or reassess your understanding of its content.

- Always look for a hint in the stem; examiners occasionally fail to eliminate these.

- Understand the key words in the questions before you attempt them.

Understanding the key words

Table 3.1 contains the typical definitions of the key words used in MCQs.

Table 3.1. Definitions of key words used in MCQs	
Key word	**Definition (what it means)**
Recognised/recognised feature/ recognised association	An acceptable feature of, irrespective of how frequent it is. What they actually mean is that the feature has been reported and it is reasonable to expect an average candidate to know it
Occurs	This has the same meaning as recognised
Essential feature	Required to confirm the diagnosis or the presence of a condition, e.g. complication
Characteristic – often used in combination as 'characteristic feature'	A feature without which the diagnosis is in question. In practice, therefore, examiners should use this rarely
Typical – again commonly used in combination with feature, as 'typical feature'	This is synonymous with characteristic
Pathognomonic	A feature specific to the disease but no other (specific to a disease or condition only and whose presence therefore is equal to identifying the condition/disease)
Specific	Same as pathognomonic
The majority or most	Means over 50%
Could/possible/may	May apply under certain circumstances. These are terms that should be avoided in MCQs as they give away the answers
Rare	Less than 5%
Almost never	1–2%
Never/always/exclusive	These words mean there are no exceptions: a very rare occurrence in medicine. Candidates should therefore be careful as examiners are aware of this and occasionally have a question where this is actually true. If you are uncertain and have to guess, you should always be reluctant to guess that the answer is true

Statistics

If you have to guess, questions that contain apparently exact statistics are often wrong. For example, a question which states that the induction rate in the UK is 30% is most likely to be wrong. This is because while this may be the case in one unit, it may be different in others. In addition, for most statistics, there are usually several studies; hence, a range is better. However, most questions will be qualified with words such as 'approximately', 'less than' or 'over' or will give a range. Candidates should also be careful, as this rule does not apply to nationally produced statistics such as those in the Confidential Enquiry into Maternal and Child Health reports. These tend to be exact as they are nationally derived (that is, from one source).

When you are guessing

There will be questions of which you are either unsure or to which you simply do not know the answer. When faced with such a question, you are advised to make an educated guess, since there is no negative marking. The following points will be helpful in improving your chances of making the correct guess.

1. The answer is likely to be **True** if the following words or phrases are used:
   a. May
   b. May be
   c. Can be
   d. Can appear
   e. Is possible
   f. Occasionally

2. The answer is likely to be **False** if the following terms or phrases are used:
   a. All
   b. Always
   c. Necessarily
   d. Is necessarily
   e. Exact statistic is used
   f. Same as
   g. Essential
   h. Never

It is important to remember that, for every rule, there is always an exception; hence, there will be questions with some of the examples (terms/phrases) given above that are either false or true. For example, 'In the latest Confidential Enquiries into Maternal Deaths in the UK 2000–2002, all direct anaesthetic deaths were in women who had been given general anaesthesia'. This is **true**, although the word 'all' was used.

Reference

1. Royal College of Obstetricians and Gynaecologists Examination Committee. *Past Papers: MRCOG Part 2 Multiple Choice Questions 1997–2001*. London: RCOG Press; 2004.

Further reading

Chen SDM. How to answer MCQs. *studentBMJ* 2005;13:89–132 [http://student. bmj.com/issues/05/03/careers/110.php].

Walsh K. Answering multiple-choice questions. *BMJ* 2005;330:228–9.

4   Part 2 Short answer question paper

History of the MRCOG essay component

The Examination Committee was formed in 1930 and the first examination for membership of the College was held the following year. Essays were first introduced to the MRCOG examination in 1967 and, in 1968, the examination was divided into two parts. Part 2 comprised clinical and viva components and the unique requirement to submit a book of case records with the essays remaining as part of the Part 2 examination. In 1997, the essay component of the Part 2 MRCOG examination changed to short-answer question format, with a specific clinical topic or problem to be dealt with. In 1998, an oral assessment replaced the clinical and viva examinations. Traditionally, there have always been ten general essays (five gynaecological and five obstetric) on medicine relevant to the practice of obstetrics and gynaecology. In 2006, the ten essays were reduced to eight, together with a reduction of the number of MCQs to allow EMQs to be introduced. In addition, the essay format was replaced by subdivided short-answer questions.

Writing the questions

Twelve to eighteen months before the examination date, a small committee of six experienced MRCOG examiners formulates a skeleton of eight proposed question topics. Generally, these topics are new to the examination, although, on occasion, old questions will be refreshed and reused, particularly on important subjects such as placenta praevia or pre-eclampsia, which of course will need to be tested from time to time. Other subjects will be selected if there has been a significant change in practice, if there has been new guidance issued or if a subject is particularly topical. The examination has never been structured as an exit examination and the standard has always been to assess an individual in the middle of their training. This has now been defined as the standard required of a typical Year 5 specialty trainee in general obstetrics and gynaecology and, hence, it is not thought appropriate to ask detailed, subspecialty-level questions.

Each committee member then works up a model answer for a particular question, although in practice this is often done in reverse, where it is easier to establish a good model answer and then design a question that will produce this answer. At the next committee meeting, the proposed question is presented without access to the model answer and the remaining five members of the committee then answer the question for real. In this way, we ensure that the question generates the correct model response. At this stage, the committee's answers are reviewed and compared with the model answer and general agreement is reached on whether the question is good enough for the examination. If general agreement cannot be obtained, then the question is discarded. The successful questions and model answers are then refined and 'polished' at committee until the finished product is reached (Figure 4.1). It has been found that the process of the committee sitting the examination blind is useful in spotting flaws in the question stems and reduces the chances of a question eliciting an alternative answer pathway. This has become more important now that the short-answer questions are broken into three or four subdivisions, where each of the individual subdivisions must stimulate the appropriate answer for that particular section.

Blueprinting

Once we have selected the eight areas of the curriculum to be covered by the SAQs, the titles are reviewed by the full Examination and Assessment Committee to enable the EMQ, MCQ and oral assessment Sub-committees to plan their questions appropriately. This allows the complete examination to be blueprinted to cover the entire syllabus. This explains why the written examination is an integral part of the oral assessment, and also why a pass in the written examination cannot be transferred to an oral assessment of a different diet. For further information on blueprinting, see Chapter 7.

How to prepare for the SAQ examination

The Part 2 MRCOG syllabus and regulations are published on the RCOG website and a suggested reading list of textbooks for the MRCOG is also available. Answers are best planned by concentrating on the key descriptive verbs (Box 4.1) and strict adherence to what the question asks will avoid wasting precious time on sections which will not gain any marks, and will allow the marks obtained from your answer to be

Question

A healthy 41-year-old nulliparous woman is considering pregnancy and wishes to know:

A. What are her risks of delivering a baby with a fetal abnormality? (3 marks)

B. How can these risks be reduced? (10 marks)

C. What risks to her own health are associated with pregnancy at her age? (5 marks)

D. Will her antenatal care be altered by her age? (2 marks)

Answer

A. What are her risks of delivering a baby with a fetal abnormality?
- All autosomal trisomies are more common in older mothers.
- The risk of T21 is approximately one in 100.
- She has normal background risk of other abnormalities, e.g. NTD/CF/CHD   **0**   **1**   **2**   **3**

B. How can these risks be reduced?

Maternal
- Highlight the importance of optimal maternal health and nutrition including the use of folic acid to reduce risk of structural abnormalities
- Stop alcohol use
- Rubella immunisations if needed   **0**   **1**   **2**   **3**

Fetal
Discuss differences between screening and diagnostic testing   **0**   **1**   **2**

Discuss the types of screening tests
- Ultrasound/nuchal test
- Serum test
- Anomaly scanning   **0**   **1**   **2**   **3**

Discuss the types of diagnostic tests
- CVS should be undertaken at no less than 10 weeks of gestation
- Amniocentesis should be undertaken at 15 weeks or greater   **0**   **1**   **2**

---

continued on the following page

Figure 4.1. Example of model SAQ answer

C. What risks to her own health are associated with pregnancy at her age?

Pregnancy at this age carries an increased risk to the mother of:

* Medical disorders of pregnancy including hypertensive, diabetes, DVT   **0**   **1**   **2**

* Multiple pregnancy
* Operative delivery
* Maternal death (all causes)   **0**   **1**   **2**   **3**

D. Will her antenatal care be altered by her age?

Other than with regard to management of chromosomal abnormalities, the management of women aged 41 years is not altered from that of younger women with the same obstetric problems. Preventive/prophylactic measures are unchanged.   **0**   **1**   **2**

References

1. Royal College of Obstetricians and Gynaecologists. Antenatal Screening for Down Syndrome. (see also www.nelh.nhs.uk/screening).
2. Royal College of Obstetricians and Gynaecologists. *Amniocentesis and Chorionic Villus Sampling*. 3rd ed. Green-top Guideline No. 8. London: RCOG; 2005 [www.rcog.org.uk/resources/Public/pdf/aminiocentesis_chorionicjan2005.pdf].
3. James DK, Steer, PJ, Weiner CP, Gonik B. *High Risk Pregnancy: Management Options*. 3rd ed. London: Saunders; 2006. Chapter 1.
4. Lewis G, editor. *Why Mothers Die 2000–2002: Sixth Report of the Confidential Enquiries into Maternal Deaths in the United Kingdom*. London: RCOG Press; 2004.

Figure 4.1. Example of model SAQ answer (continued)

maximised. If each of your first three essays over-runs by as little as 4 minutes, then you have used up 40% of the time available for the last question. It is essential that every question should be attempted. The quality of the content of your answer is more important than the length and it is well attested that many high-scoring answers are contained well within the allocated space. The use of headings, underlining and highlighting with coloured inks is acceptable and will help to emphasise important points or key words. However, these are not mandatory. There is no penalty for incorrect spelling or poor grammar as long as the intended meaning is clear. However, it is important that your writing is legible. A formal introduction and conclusion are not essential and can indeed waste valuable time without gaining marks.

BOX 4.1. VERBS USED IN CONSTRUCTING SHORT-ANSWER QUESTIONS

DESCRIPTOR VERBS:

- Describe
- Define
- Identify
- Explain
- Demonstrate

- Categorise
- Compare
- Contrast
- Distinguish

- Justify
- Critique
- Criticise
- Prioritise

Verbs/terms used to demonstrate knowledge, comprehension, analysis and evaluation of facts:

- Critically evaluate
- Justify
- Pros and cons
- Patient management
- Situation management

How to answer SAQs

Assuming that your preparation has been adequate, the topics of the short answer questions should not come as a surprise. It is important to read the question extremely carefully. The questions are carefully written to exclude any extraneous, irrelevant or misleading words. If a word is in the question, then it is important and it is there for a reason. There are no trick questions. A good thought process is to imagine the patient in the question sitting in front of you in your clinic: what would you say and do?

As you read the question, also look at the number of marks that are allocated to each of the sub-sections, as this will guide you as to how much time you should spend on each of the sections. If, for example, there are only two marks for section D, then the vast majority of your time should be spent on Sections A–C, which garner 18 marks. After you have read the question, it is important to take 3–5 minutes to plan your answer on the rough paper provided. Only after this stage should you begin to write. If you do not plan, then you will forget things or else you will remember later and put information in the wrong place. It is important to try to write in prose using good English with correct spelling and not to use lists, abbreviations or bullet points. The questions are framed in such a way that marks will not be given just for a one-word answer but rather for explaining or justifying the reasons. Marks are not usually given just for giving a list of investigations; the question usually asks for justification; for example, to give the reason why you would request a particular investigation involving a patient's management. 'Soft' marks are not generally given for mentioning history and examination, taking consent, giving a patient information leaflet or filling in a critical incident form. These are now considered standard practice and the marks are awarded for critical evaluation above and beyond these basic skills.

While you are writing the answer you should revisit the question that was asked and make sure that you answer only what was asked. Too often when we are marking the answers, we see the use of a 'grapeshot' technique of simply writing down everything known about a particular topic. This will rarely gain many marks.

It is also extremely important to finish all questions by the end of the allocated time. It is virtually impossible to pass this paper if you answer only seven of the questions, so it is paramount that you treat each question as you do in an OSCE. When the time allocated for each question is up, you move on and start afresh with the next one. Similarly, we recommend that you take the questions in order rather than picking the easy ones first and saving the more difficult ones to the end because you will risk running out of time. It is essential, after 26 minutes, to move on to the next question, regardless. If you have a few minutes at the end, then of course it is appropriate to go back and re-read your answers and to polish any rough edges.

KNOWLEDGE

Knowledge, experience and practice, probably in equal measures, are required to succeed in the SAQs. With regard to knowledge, an appreciation of the current evidence-based practice in the UK is required. Although the committee uses clinical experience, this now tends to be backed by evidence-based medicine. Box 4.2 gives some examples of sources used when setting questions.

BOX 4.2. SOME SOURCES USED IN QUESTION SETTING

RCOG sources:
- *BJOG* [www.blackwellpublishing.com/bjog]
- *The Obstetrician & Gynaecologist* (TOG) [www.rcog.org.uk/togonline]
- Green-top Guidelines [www.rcog.org.uk/index.asp?PageID=1042]
- Consent guidance [www.rcog.org.uk/index.asp?PageID=686]
- Ethical hot topics [www.rcog.org.uk/index.asp?PageID=845]
- Scientific Opinion Papers [www.rcog.org.uk/index.asp?PageID=80]
- National Evidence-based Clinical Guidelines [www.rcog.org.uk/index.asp?PageID=1046]
- Study Group Consensus Statements [www.rcog.org.uk/index.asp?PageID=82]
- Working Party Reports [www.rcog.org.uk/index.asp?PageID=1167]

Other organisations:
- Faculty of Sexual Health and Reproductive Health Care [www.ffprhc.org.uk, under 'Publications']
- National Institute for Health and Clinical Excellence (NICE) [http://guidance.nice.org.uk/topic/gynaecology]
- Scottish Intercollegiate Guidelines Network (SIGN) [www.sign.ac.uk/guidelines/index.html]

Other journals:
- *BMJ*
- *The Lancet*
- *American Journal of Obstetrics and Gynecology*

EXPERIENCE

Many of the questions require situational awareness where you are an intermediate specialty trainee (ST3, ST4 or ST5) in charge of the labour ward or in the operating theatre and, hence, sitting the paper during your basic specialty training (ST1 or ST2) can prove difficult if you have not experienced these situations. When preparing and writing your answers, try to think of yourself as an intermediate trainee and act appropriately. Questions are not set with any tricks or tripwires and we do not expect consultant-level decisions or subspecialty skills.

PRACTICE

No matter how good your knowledge and experience, unless you practise writing essays in English you will struggle when it comes to the examination. It is important that you make your practice as frequent and as realistic as possible. Following study guides or, with the use of a study group or tutor, you should be aiming to write at least two SAQs per week. Consider asking your tutor to pick an essay and then seal it in an envelope, which should be kept closed until you are sitting at your desk. You then open the envelope, plan the answer and write your answer using two sides of A4 paper for a total of 26 minutes. It is important not to cheat by checking your answer in a textbook or taking longer than the specified time, as this will only lead to a false sense of security. By repeatedly doing this, you will cover the syllabus and gain confidence in your ability to write focused answers in the allotted time. It is important that you remain focused with a clear, structured answer and this can best be achieved by continually re-reading the question.

Where possible it is best to prepare by working in the UK, as British practice can be different from that in other parts of the world. Once you know how the British system works and, in particular, approaches to patients, relatives and staff, the questions become easier to answer.

How to revise and when to sit the examination

The SAQs are not just about writing an essay on a particular topic. They are an examination of how you use your knowledge and, because clinical medicine is not always a straightforward exercise in logic, we frequently ask candidates to debate the 'pros and cons' of a condition or a particular clinical situation. We may ask candidates to justify the management of certain conditions using information derived from the evidence base.

The RCOG Green-top Guidelines and information are easily accessible on the College website. All trainees are offered one free introductory tutorial in the College's interactive online distance learning programme, StratOG.net, on joining the Trainees' Register. You are highly recommended to access this tutorial and to take advantage of this comprehensive training programme (www.stratog.net).

There are other practical and internet courses available, as well as MRCOG online 'blogs' and study groups. Like all revision aids, they will vary in quality and educational methods. Do your research and find a well-recommended course that suits your needs. Finally, it is important not to sit the examination too early but to wait until you and your supervisors think you are ready. The best time to pass is at your first attempt.

Getting through the examination

Box 4.3 gives some practical tips for ensuring that you give yourself the best chance to make the most of the examination.

It is vital that you read the instructions and obey them. The general instructions to candidates are shown in Box 4.4.

How the short answers are marked

What happens after you have written your answer? Firstly, all the scripts are sealed and returned to the RCOG where they are anonymised and randomised. This means that, when the script is being marked, it only has your candidate number at the top. Scripts from throughout the world are in random order so that each examiner will not be aware of who they are marking, nor will the examiner mark scripts from only a single centre. Any script could be from any of the 15 MRCOG centres throughout the world.

Approximately 10 days after the written examination, a group of senior examiners meets at the College, where they are divided into marking groups of 12. To ensure a consistent approach to the marking, each group will mark all the answers from a particular question. For example, table A of 12 examiners will mark all the questions that have been submitted for question 1 and table B will mark all the scripts from question 2, and so on.

A senior examiner experienced in the examination process is allocated to chair each team of markers. The first hour of the meeting is spent discussing three sample questions to ensure inter-rater reliability and to reduce variability. The examiners then agree the model answer scheme supplied by the SAQ Sub-committee and they will aim to give the same scores on the three sample questions. The chairperson of each question will mediate until agreement is reached and will determine when marks should and should not be awarded. Very occasionally, the marking sheet is modified and the revised sheet will then be returned to the SAQ Sub-committee for use in any future examinations.

BOX 4.3. PRACTICAL TIPS FOR THE EXAMINATION

Day before the examination
Exercise, fresh air and good night's sleep.

On the day
Ensure that you know the location and start time.

Arrive well before time, even the night before if travelling a long distance.

Arrive early and unstressed.

Photographic ID and RCOG registration.

Bottled water.

Telephones and PDAs are not allowed in the examination hall, so will be collected before admission, or leave behind.

Pen (plus spare) and a watch.

Check the instructions.

Read the questions carefully.

Read both sides.

Plan your answer.

Imagine you have this patient in front of you at the clinic in the UK.

In summary:
✔ **Open**
✔ **Read**
✔ **Plan**
✔ **Write**
✔ **Read**
✔ **Write**
✔ **Finish on time!**

The marking then starts in earnest and, throughout the rest of the day, each examiner will mark individual answer sheets and marks are then transferred on to a computer record sheet. Each completed mark sheet is crosschecked by a co-examiner who is marking the same question to ensure that the structured mark sheets have been completed correctly, the arithmetical calculations are correct and each candidate's score has been correctly transferred to the computer sheet.

Throughout the day, for the purposes of quality control and to ensure consistency, the chairperson for each table will read samples of marked scripts from all of the examiners at the table. Each SAQ has a total of 20 marks to be awarded and no half-marks are used. These marks are highlighted in the structured answer (Figure 4.2).

For each SAQ, a maximum of two marks may be deducted for persistent factual errors and a further four for dangerous clinical practice. Examples of this will be provided on the mark sheet. For example, the use of radiotherapy in the treatment of a hydatidiform mole would be regarded as dangerous practice. If a candidate scores extremely poorly, or if marks are to be removed for dangerous clinical practice, then moderators from the SAQ Sub-committee will double-mark the question before a final mark is agreed.

In total, over 100 senior examiners give up a full day for marking and we are grateful for their dedication, energy and enthusiasm in this process. It is important to understand the human element when you are writing a short-answer question and to appreciate how difficult it is for examiners to mark when a script is poorly written or illegible (Figure 4.3).

PART 2 MRCOG MARCH 2007

CANDIDATE NUMBER

QUESTION 1:

A woman presents with light vaginal bleeding at 37 weeks. She has had two previous caesarean sections. An earlier ultrasound suggests the placenta is anterior and low.

A. Describe how your initial assessment would help you to establish the correct diagnosis: (10 marks)

B. Justify what investigations will be useful in her further management: (7 marks)

C. What specific intra-operative complications should this woman be advised about before her caesarean section? (3 marks)

A. Specific history
- History of contractions – suggests labour / minor abruption
- Pain present – suggests abruption / rupture; lack of pain – suggests praevia
- Onset and amount of blood loss (? Show)
- History of abnormal cervical smear – may suggest cervical cause
- Absent / reduced fetal movements – suggests abruption / rupture   0 1 2 3 4 5

Examination
- Assessment of maternal condition (signs of shock suggests concealed abruption or rupture)
- Abdominal palpation
  - Abnormal fetal lie (placenta praevia or rupture)
  - Fetal parts felt easily (rupture)
  - Uterine tenderness (abruption or rupture)
- Avoid vaginal examination until placenta praevia excluded   0 1 2 3 4 5

B. Investigations

Maternal:
- Ultrasound for placenta location
- Ultrasound is not specific / helpful in diagnosing abruption
- MRI may be helpful (placenta accreta / percreta)   0 1 2 3

- Full blood count & coagulation screen – may be abnormal in abruption
- Kleihauer – would indicate significant fetomaternal haemorrhage   0 1 2

Fetal:
- CTG
- Identify fetal blood in vagina eg Apt's test / Kleihauer   0 1 2

C. Complicatons
- Bladder injury
- Haemorrhage
- Hysterectomy   0 1 2 3

Add up marks   /20

In exceptional circumstances you may deduct marks for
   persistent factual error (> 3)   0 1 2

   dangerous clinical practice   0 1 2 3 4
   (scan for abruption / VE before scan)

Final Score   /20

Figure 4.2. Structured answer and mark plan

Question Number 4   Candidate number

A previously healthy 32-year-old has had a normal vaginal delivery of her fourth baby. You are crash-bleeped to attend her on the postnatal ward because of acute severe chest pain and shortness of breath.

A. Justify the key aspects of your initial assessment: (10 marks)

PE is the leading first leading cause
of maternal death. D-D Δ MI - Amniotic Embolism
pt Resuscitation is the first thing to do AB
Airway - oxygen Respiration & Circulation maintain
call for Cardiac team & resuscitation
I.V. line Att MoNa
Att
& O₂
< Thrombolytic p. Streptokinase

A. (continued)   Question Number 4

B. How would your bedside investigations develop your differential diagnosis? (3 marks)

EC.G st Inverted ST segment n MI
P.E Q₃⁵ - S wave up D lead 7
pulse oxymetry hypoxemia in P-E
D dimer Not useful in pregnancy Ventilation
Ventilation perfusion

C. Outline your continuing management plan: (7 marks)

Thrombolytic = Aspirin
Att Isordil

surgical -

[END OF PAPER]

Please ensure your **candidate number** is on the top of the answer sheet.

Figure 4.3. Example of an inadequate answer

54 A GUIDE TO THE EXAMINATION

A standard-setting process is undertaken for each part of the examination and the overall pass mark is established for each examination, depending on its difficulty. If the examination is relatively easy, the pass mark goes up; if it is harder the pass mark goes down (see Chapter 7 for a full account of the standard setting process).

In the past, one or two discretionary marks were used if the examiner thought that the candidate had written a particularly 'good' answer. This practice has now been discontinued, as it was considered to be too subjective and was hard to standardise.

While the SAQs are set according to the Part 2 MRCOG Syllabus, there are certain areas, such as surgical skills, which are better explored in an OSCE. The SAQs will aim to examine the decision-making processes around when to carry out a particular operation or to deal with a particular complication.

SAQ KEY POINTS

- SAQs give character and depth to the MRCOG examination.
- The format tests medical and clinical knowledge, critical judgement, attitudes and diagnostic skills.
- It requires an approach based on good clinical knowledge and an ability to reflect on a question and to create a logical answer that addresses the points raised in the various parts of the question.
- The separation of the SAQs into subsections has proved popular and prevents candidates writing a whole answer to the 'wrong' question.
- The questions are drawn from the breadth of the Syllabus
- A candidate writing to the level of a UK specialty registrar (previously termed a specialist registrar) in obstetrics and gynaecology should be able to attain a pass.

5 Part 2 Extended matching question paper

Introduction

The RCOG is continually reviewing the format of the Part 2 Membership examination to take account of current evidence and thinking, to provide an assessment tool that is up to date, relevant, appropriate and fair. Extended matching questions have, over recent years, been widely used in undergraduate and, more recently, postgraduate medical examinations. Educationalists feel that they are a very good assessment of a candidate's ability and a very good discriminator between the good and not so good candidate.[1] Modern psychometric methods indicate that the reliability of EMQ papers is particularly good[2] and, furthermore, a recent literature review of question formats in medical examinations concluded that 'there is a wealth of evidence that EMQs are the fairest format'.[3]

In light of this, the RCOG set up a Working Party in 2003 (at that point a sub-group of the MCQ Sub-committee), to assess the feasibility of introducing an EMQ paper into the Part 2 MRCOG written examination. Over the next 2 years, the group (by then renamed the EMQ Sub-committee) produced over 500 questions that had been subject to rigorous editing and were thought to be at the correct level for the Part 2 examination. This, of course, like all parts of the paper, is based on the expected level of knowledge of an average Year 5 specialty trainee. In 2005, an initial paper was piloted internally at the College. This was a success and, after a full assessment of the results of this trial, the RCOG Council ratified the introduction of EMQs to the Part 2 MRCOG examination. The EMQ paper has thus been part of the written examination since September 2006.

Evaluative benefits of an EMQ paper

True/false MCQs remain a valid part of the Part 2 MRCOG examination, as they are a thorough test of factual knowledge (see Chapter 3).[4] This continues to be recognised as the single best determinant of expertise in any subject.[3] A further benefit of MCQs is that they are objective and can be marked by computer. This has the clear advantage of being 100% accurate and is also extremely time efficient. There are, however, downsides to this mode of testing. Firstly, MCQs predominantly test recall and not the application of knowledge. Hence, someone who has a very good memory but who is not necessarily a good practitioner will still score very highly. Secondly, candidates may be able to get the right answer by elimination rather than by actual knowledge. Although the College has constantly reviewed its MCQ paper, tried to make it clinically relevant and to avoid obscure or isolated facts, it is still the case that an EMQ paper has an advantage over MCQs alone.

The short-answer questions compensate for the pitfalls of the MCQ paper to some extent, inasmuch as they require candidates to demonstrate their critical understanding of current topics in obstetrics and gynaecology (see chapter 4). In the past, candidates would be left to surmise exactly what was required of them and what would be rewarded with marks. Essays require the candidate to write in well-constructed English – something which some international candidates found difficult and which was possibly not a test of medical competence.[5] However, as the benchmark for the Part 2 MRCOG is set at the level of a UK year 5 specialty trainee, it is reasonable to include a test of ability to communicate in written English, since this remains an essential skill for doctors writing in medical notes. The short answer paper allows candidates to express themselves in some depth and tests areas of reasoning that cannot properly be assessed using a multiple-choice or EMQ format. Marking is demanding of manpower and time and must inevitably have a degree of subjectivity. To reduce subjectivity as much as possible and to make it easier for candidates to construct their answers, the SAQ Sub-committee has recently introduced subdivisions into the SAQs, which have allowed for a more detailed and 'easy to follow' mark scheme. This innovation has proven popular with both candidates and examiners. The educational validity of the short answer question remains controversial[6] and the Examination and Assessment Committee will continue to review the structure of this part of the examination on a regular basis.

Educational research clearly shows that the greater number of formats an examination possesses, the greater number of performance indicators one is assessing and the fairer the examination is.[7] The introduction of EMQs achieves several evaluative functions. An EMQ is a variant of the true/false response MCQ but contains many more different options, usually between 10 and 16, with the candidate having to choose the single most appropriate option to gain a mark. Guessing, therefore, is much less likely to result in a positive outcome.

The EMQ tests the application of medical knowledge rather than simple recall and so more complex understanding is tested. Close comparison in trials to all other question formats demonstrates that EMQs can examine clinical problem-solving particularly well.[1] Compared with the short-answer format, EMQs allow a greater number of subjects and domains to be covered, with any paper covering between 14 and 20 topics. Inevitably, the EMQ paper will most typically deal with the domains of investigation, diagnosis and management but it also lends itself to the testing of areas such as data interpretation, audit, statistics, epidemiology and genetics. In addition, the EMQ paper has all the benefits of computer marking, primarily the avoidance of examiner bias.

The addition of the EMQ format allows greater coverage of the syllabus and this, plus the 'blueprinting' of the four papers (see chapter 7), goes a long way towards avoidance of overemphasis of a few segments, thus increasing the reliability and validity of the whole Part 2 examination.[8]

Structure of EMQs

An EMQ is composed of three parts:

- a list of options
- a lead-in statement
- a number of twigs (questions).

OPTION LIST

The list of options (typically between 10 and 14) is the 'answer' list. One of these options is the correct answer for each twig or question. Depending on the type of question, the option list may be possible management options, diagnoses, surgical options, statistical tests, numbers (for instance, percentages), clinical complications or potential treatments, to cite a few examples.

The greater the number of options the more daunting the question may be. Although there is some evidence that the more options there are, the more comprehensive is the testing of a candidate's abilities, do not be put off. Often, in a big list of options, there are simply more distractors or answers that cannot be true for any one twig or question.

LEAD-IN STATEMENT

The lead-in statement is critical to the question and must be read very carefully, as this is your direct instruction as to what you are being asked to do. Sometimes this will be a very short and bland statement, such as 'for each clinical scenario described below choose the single most appropriate management from the above list of options'. Sometimes, however, it will be much lengthier and contain a lot of clinical information, about a clinical situation to which all of the twigs or questions will apply. This could start, for example: 'Each of the clinical scenarios below refer to a 61-year-old patient who has recently undergone abdominal hysterectomy, BSO and colposacropexy for severe uterine prolapse. The operation took longer than expected, as there were extensive adhesions to bowel and pelvic sidewalls. For each clinical scenario described below choose the single...'. In such a question, this clinical information will not be repeated in each twig, so it is imperative that the candidate reads the statement carefully otherwise they may easily misunderstand the question.

TWIGS (QUESTIONS)

Clearly, the questions will vary hugely, depending upon the theme of the question and which domain is being assessed. Themes, for example, can be anything from the whole range of topics covered in the syllabus; that is, fetal and maternal medicine, pelvic pain, reproductive medicine, benign gynaecology, and so on. Domain relates to the area of that topic is being studied: for instance, clinical genetics, treatment, investigation, epidemiology, and so on. Examples of questions or twigs therefore would typically be a clinical scenario but could also be a description of a virus or drug, a set of clinical results, findings on ultrasound.

In the examination, there will almost always be either two or three twigs per option list. It would be very unusual to have only one twig for an option list and to have four or more twigs per option list (on one topic) would limit the number of areas that could be studied in one 40-twig examination paper, as well as perhaps putting too much emphasis on one subject.

Although EMQ writing is well recognised as being technically difficult, the College has made every effort to produce a bank of questions that are clear, easily read and unambiguous. The list of options is homogeneous and each option is as short as possible. The lead-in statement gives a clear indication of what is required of the candidate. The questions may be long if a scenario is depicted but vagueness and ambiguous statements are avoided.

Each EMQ is edited three times before being added to the bank and is re-edited before being included in a paper to ensure that it remains appropriate and up to date.

Examples

EXAMPLE 1

The theme of Example 1 (Figure 5.1) is urogynaecology and is from the domain of management. The list of options comprises 14 treatments that could be reasonably employed in the management of pelvic organ prolapse. Although there are surgical and nonsurgical options, the list is homogeneous, as they are all clearly treatments employed for prolapse and nothing else. There are not, for example, options that are solely treatments of say, menstrual disorders or overactive bladder. The lead-in statement is brief and clear, with no clinical information within it. The questions are also relatively brief but contain enough clinical information to allow the candidate with an appropriate level of knowledge about pelvic organ prolapse to answer correctly.

In question 1, the candidate needs to recognise that the patient is a poor surgical risk and therefore a conservative management option is likely to be the answer. The patient described has marked pelvic organ prolapse, so physiotherapy will not be able to deal with it and the age of the patient is against successful physiotherapy treatment. The options are thus between a shelf pessary and a ring pessary and the candidate needs to know that the latter is more successful where there is uterine prolapse, and so in this case the answer is I – Shelf pessary. Minimal surgical treatment such as Le Fort's procedure or colpocleisis could be an option for management in this patient **but it is not on the list of options**. It is not unusual when constructing questions to exclude one treatment option from the list of options when there are two equally appropriate treatments for a situation.

In question 2, the candidate will need to know that patients who have had a previous colposuspension are very prone to later posterior vaginal wall prolapse. The other information provided is all in keeping with a rectocele as the diagnosis. The fact that the bulge is visible again excludes physiotherapy as a successful treatment; therefore, the answer is G – Posterior repair.

In question 3, the candidate is being pointed towards the fact that this is a young woman still of childbearing age, who has recently been pregnant and who has relatively mild symptoms and a mild degree of prolapse on examination. The candidate needs to know that her problems may well respond to physiotherapy treatment, and that surgical treatment should ideally only be done when child bearing is complete. With the information available therefore, the most appropriate management option is N – pelvic floor physiotherapy.

OPTIONS

A   Anterior repair

B   Anterior repair and Kelly's sutures

C   Anterior repair and sub urethral tape

D   Colposacropexy

E   Enterocele repair

F   Paravaginal repair

G   Posterior repair

H   Ring pessary

I   Shelf pessary

J   Vaginal hysterectomy

K   Vaginal hysterectomy and anterior repair

L   Vaginal hysterectomy, anterior repair and Kelly's sutures

M   Colposuspension

N   Pelvic floor physiotherapy Instructions

INSTRUCTIONS

For each case, described below choose the single most appropriate management from the above list of options. Each option may be used once, more than once or not at all.

Question 1
An 83-year-old woman presents with a significant bulge vaginally, which is visible at the introitus. It is rubbing on her underwear and causing light bleeding. She had a vaginal hysterectomy and anterior repair 16 years ago. She has had three myocardial infarctions in the last 18 months and is in mild CCF. She desperately wants something done, as she is very uncomfortable.

Question 2
A 56-year-old woman had a colposuspension 8 years ago for stress incontinence. She now presents with a vaginal bulge and discomfort. She has some voiding difficulty and occasional urinary tract infections. She has noticed recently she has to digitate the vagina to help empty her bowel.

Question 3
A 36-year-old woman complains of occasional stress incontinence and a feeling of vaginal pressure. She is a para 2 and during her recent pregnancy she had some stress incontinence. On examination, she has a mild to moderate cystocele.

Figure 5.1. Example 1

EXAMPLE 2

The theme of Example 2 (Figure 5.2) is intrapartum care and the domain is diagnosis. The list of options contains 15 conditions that are related to maternal collapse in the intrapartum period. The lead-in statement in this example contains quite a bit of information relating to the clinical scenario to which each question will relate and this information must be borne in mind when answering each twig. Each twig provides further clinical information about the patient and describes a clinical event. This extra information and the account of the event should fairly readily lead the candidate to the right answer.

In question 1, the fact that the patient is a smoker may raise several options as to the possible cause, but the clue to the answer is in the examination findings. From the option list only a tension pneumothorax will give the finding of **significant** reduced air entry.

In question 2, the fact that she is a non-smoker is pointing you away from certain problems but, again, the diagnosis is worked out from the clinical scenario. The absence of bleeding rules out haemorrhage and, as the placenta is being delivered, abruption is not an option. The fact that she has previously been well rules out many of the options and the timing of the collapse (with delivery of the placenta) is classical of an amniotic fluid embolism, which is the correct answer.

In question 3, the added information given describes clear risk factors for thromboembolism and the clinical picture is classical of a patient developing a pulmonary thromboembolism and subsequently collapsing from it.

Approaches to answering an EMQ

As with any examination format, it is imperative to read the question very carefully, as failure to do so may lead the candidate to miss vital information leading to a wrong answer. In a stressful examination situation it is easy to misread the question. This is most likely to be avoided if you take a deep breath to calm yourself, read the question slowly and read it twice.

Traditionally, the option list is given first in an EMQ and the College has decided to stick with this format. You should, however, read the lead-in statement (instructions) first and ignore the option list to begin with. Next, having established that you are clear about what you are being asked to do, you should proceed to read the first question very carefully. You should work out your answer and **then** go to the option list for the first time to find it. If it is there, then mark your answer on the answer sheet and move to the next question. If it is **not** there, then

OPTIONS

A Amniotic fluid embolism

B Cardiomyopathy

C Chest infection

D Cerebrovascular accident

E Deep venous thrombosis

F Endocarditis

G Haemorrhage

H HELLP syndrome

I Myocardial infarction

J Placental abruption

K Pulmonary embolism

L Pulmonary hypertension

M Sepsis

N Substance misuse

O Tension pneumothorax Instructions

INSTRUCTIONS

Each of the cases below relates to a 40-year-old woman who was admitted in spontaneous labour earlier in the day. Initial examination in the labour ward showed her to be 5 cm dilated and a cardiotocograph was normal. Her pregnancy had been entirely uneventful. For each case choose the single most likely diagnosis from the above list of options. Each option may be used once, more than once or not at all.

Question 1
This woman is a heavy smoker and is in her third pregnancy. Two hours after admission she complains of chest pain and breathlessness. On sounding her chest there is significantly reduced air entry on the right side.

Question 2
This colleague's partner is a primigravida and a non-smoker. She labours without complication. She has a normal delivery and as the placenta is being delivered she collapses. There is no excessive bleeding.

Question 3
This woman is markedly obese and is in her sixth pregnancy. Soon after admission she develops dyspnoea and pain on taking a deep breath. Auscultation of the chest suggests a possible reduction in air entry in the middle lobe on the right-hand side. Before further assessment can be made she collapses.

Figure 5.2. Example 2

re-read the question. The reason it is not there is either that you have misread the question, or your assessment is wrong, or your assessment is correct but that answer is not there, in which case you need to pick the next most appropriate answer.

Start at the beginning of the paper and work your way through steadily to the end. Do not pick out questions you think you know a lot about and answer them first, as this then leaves you under pressure for the questions you may know less about. Be aware of time. There are 40 questions (twigs) to be answered in an hour so you have one and a half minutes for each, and this is ample time. From March 2008, the Part 2 MCQ and EMQ papers are distributed together, so candidates are able to allocate their time to the two papers as they wish within the limit of 2 hours 45 minutes. Very few candidates run out of time but if you are falling behind time then speed up. If you are extremely confused about one EMQ (which should be very unlikely) then leave it and come back to it. Make sure you answer all 40 questions, even if you are not sure of the answer or if you run out of time, because there is no negative marking.

As with all of the examination formats, practise answering this particular type of question as much as you can, as there is good evidence that increasing familiarity with any format improves performance.[1] Further examples of EMQs are provided on the College website and there are now several books of practice EMQs available. A comprehensive guide to EMQs, with worked examples and practice papers for you to complete, is published by the RCOG.[9]

The future of the EMQ paper

At the time of writing, there have so far been three sittings of the EMQ paper and the Examination and Assessment Committee has been very pleased with the performance of these three papers. The performance has shown EMQs in the setting of the Part 2 examination to be good discriminators, with the vast majority of questions being answered correctly by those who do well overall and less so by those who do not. The current situation of 40 twigs will be the format for at least the next two sittings of the examination and possibly longer. However, in response to feedback from some candidates who struggled with the time allocated to the EMQ component of the examination, the duration of the EMQ paper has been increased for future examinations. It may well be that, if the paper continues to prove itself to be a good discriminator, the length of the paper and therefore the overall weight of the EMQ portion of the written examination may increase. However, it is unlikely in the foreseeable future that either of the other two formats – the short-answer questions or the MCQs – will be entirely replaced by EMQs.

References

1. Beullens J, Van Damme B, Jaspaert H, Janssen PJ. Are extended matching multiple-choice items appropriate for a final test in medical education? *Medical Teacher* 2002;24:390–5.
2. Bhakta B, Tennant A, Horton M, Lawton G, Andrich D. Using item response theory to explore the psychometric properties of extended matching questions examination in undergraduate medical education. *BMC Med Educ* 2004;38:803–4.
3. McCoubrie P. Improving the fairness of multiple-choice questions: a literature review. *Medical Teacher* 2004;76;709–12.
4. Downing SM, Baranowski RA, Grosso LJ, Norcini JJ. Item type and cognitive ability measured: the validity evidence for multiple true-false items in medical speciality specification. *Applied Measurement in Education* 1995;8:187–97.
5. Stobart G. Fairness in multicultural assessment systems. *Assessment in Education* 2005;12:275–87.
6. Schuwirth LW, van der Vleuten CP. ABC of learning and teaching in medicine: written assessment. *BMJ* 2003;326:643–5.
7. Linn RL. Assessments and accountability. *Educational Researcher* 2000;29:4–12.
8. Schuwirth LW, van der Vleuten CP. Changing education, changing assessment, changing research? *Med Educ* 2004;38:803–4.
9. Duthie J, Hodges P. *EMQs for the MRCOG Part 2*. London: RCOG Press; 2006.

6   The oral assessment

Introduction

In the Part 2 MRCOG examination, the oral assessment, an objective structured clinical examination (OSCE), has taken over the role of the clinical part of the assessment. The written part of the examination is the formal test of factual knowledge and those who proceed to the oral assessment should have the ability to pass it. The oral assessment should be regarded as a test of the application of that knowledge in a series of different settings. There is no carry-over of marks from the written papers and, as a consequence, it should be considered as a 'stand alone' examination. The candidate needs to pass both parts of the examination in order to be awarded the MRCOG.

In the past, a candidate would see and present one gynaecological patient and an obstetric one, be observed examining her and then have a viva voce as the clinical part of the examination. The range and complexity of the patients were not standardised and the assessment of clinical examination skills should now be part of structured training. The vivas were also of varying standard and frequently reflected the vagaries of the examiners. The oral assessment avoids any perceived or inherent unfairness or bias by standardising the questions with every candidate answering exactly the same question on that particular day of the examination irrespective of venue.

Setting the questions

A sub-committee consisting of eight Fellows or Members of the College sets the questions during the 6 months leading up to the examination. The sub-committee members are drawn from all over the UK. They have complementary interests, which helps to ensure that the questions are not too complex or aimed at an inappropriate level. The questions are aimed at what would be expected clinically of a specialty registrar year 5 (StR5). The questions are written by the sub-committee members individually and then edited in a plenary session. The aim is to make the questions, instructions and mark sheets as straightforward as possible to avoid ambiguity and to ensure there are no 'catches' in them. Each question has a 'partner' one, which is similar but not exactly the same, that is used on the second day of the examination. The sub-committee also aims to ensure that the examiner's structured mark sheet reflects the tasks that the candidate is instructed to undertake.

Blueprinting

The aim of the MRCOG is to acknowledge the attainment of a level of knowledge and experience commensurate with that expected of an StR 5. It is therefore important that the examination covers as much of the syllabus/curriculum as possible. To achieve this coverage, the chairs of the Part 2 MRCOG MCQ, SAQ, EMQ and the Oral Assessment Sub-committees compile a blueprint to ensure that there is no duplication between the components. Occasionally, duplication may be inevitable and there may be some overlap, but care is taken to avoid this occurrence. As a consequence, the examination should be seen to test that breadth of knowledge and its application. Consequently, each time a candidate sits the examination, both the written and oral components of the same diet must be completed, as the content of the two sections changes from one sitting to the next. This is one of the reasons why the RCOG does not give exemptions to candidates who have passed the written paper but failed the oral assessment.

Content of the oral assessment

The logistics of the examination day will be dealt with later but, essentially, the candidate will be marked on ten stations. These can be divided into:

• role-playing stations where an actor plays the part of a patient
• interactive stations with the examiner.

Recently, the circuits have consisted of five interactive stations and five with a role player. Each station is marked out of 20. It is not essential to pass all the stations or one in particular. An overall pass mark is needed in the oral assessment to obtain the MRCOG. The pass mark usually ranges between 115 and 120 and this variation will be discussed in the standard setting section.

Role-playing stations

At this type of station, the candidate will meet a professional actress who will play the part of a patient. Occasionally, a male role player may be used. Each station will have a set of instructions setting out the scenario, with a series of bullet points at the end. Candidates will be marked on their ability to address those points. The examiner will be a 'fly on the wall'; they will take no part in the station apart from scoring the candidate. No further information other than that provided by the role player will be available. If examination findings are given in the instructions, then that is exactly what the question is testing. Take those findings as being true; if a part of the physical examination is not included, then ask the role player, who will have been given appropriate instructions, to deal with the situation depending on its relevance. Otherwise, you can safely assume that the examination findings are normal; likewise with test results. It is important for the candidate to appreciate that the appearance of the role player may not correspond exactly to the patient they are simulating. Hence, the need to read the question instructions, especially with regard to age, body mass index and the like. The role players may also have a series of questions that will need to be addressed, or a series of prompts to keep the candidate on the right track.

The types of questions that will involve the role player include:

- **history taking**: this is a core skill and consequently will be included in every examination. It surprising that, although one would expect this type of station to be a highly scoring one, the reverse is true. Essential elements of the history are omitted, which very often leads to the subsequent parts of the question being poorly answered. In the UK, midwives undertake most obstetric booking histories and this may reflect the poor performance of many candidates. In preparation, the candidate is advised to appraise the limitations of their own history taking.

- **breaking bad news**: bad news can be simply defined as information that the patient is not expecting. There will usually be a station dealing with this aspect of patient care. The candidate should understand that there would be no doubt about the diagnosis in the majority of questions. In obstetrics, the usual scenario may involve a fetal abnormality picked up on an ultrasound scan, which may or may not be incompatible with extrauterine life, the loss of a fetal heart or the need to deliver early. In gynaecology, the bad news may be a diagnosis of cancer, precancer or the inability to become pregnant. Whichever scenario is used, the candidate is advised to think of management options that may be given to the role player.

Two useful pieces of advice for this type of station are:

○ use diagrams to explain diagnoses and options

○ allow the role player time to ask questions. In other words, to accept silences, however uncomfortable they may feel.

- **counselling a patient/discussing a diagnosis and/or treatment options**: this type of station may involve a preparatory station with a set of notes for the patient. It may involve: debriefing the role player after an untoward incident while in hospital; discussing clinical results and subsequent management options open to the patient. It cannot be emphasised enough that the candidate needs to read the question and to address the appropriate bullet points. A major pitfall with this type of question is that the candidate reverts to the comfort zone of history taking and does not address the issues in the question.

- **communicating/interpreting information**: a common type of this scenario will involve the patient bringing in information from the internet to discuss concerning her further management options. A preparatory station is usual to allow the candidate to read and assess the information. The information will be relevant to the tasks required in the question.

- **practical skills/teaching**: teaching is part of the curriculum and is best assessed in an OSCE setting. A good exercise for candidates to prepare for this type of question is to teach medical students or doctors junior to themselves. If a skill is being demonstrated, candidates need to demonstrate that skill, to take the role player through it and then to ask them to undertake it alone.

Interactive vivas with the examiner

The types of question that will involve only the examiner and the candidate include:

- **prioritisation exercise**: usually there will be a preparatory station to go through the information before meeting the examiner. In obstetrics, this may be a labour ward board to assess; in gynaecology, it may be a waiting list. It is important that, irrespective of the candidate's approach to the question, no case is omitted. The examiners are advised not to prompt and marks will therefore not be awarded to cases that the candidate has not discussed. The candidate needs to understand the meanings of NHS target times. Target waits refer to suspected cancers and a diagnosis needs to be made within 31 days of referral and treatment commenced within 62 days. Urgent wait means within 4–6 weeks and routine wait is 18 weeks from being placed on the waiting list. This may change again with continuing NHS reforms.

- **interpreting results**: the candidate may be required to consider what further information is necessary, giving a diagnosis or discussing further management options. The results for the most part will be straightforward with no hidden catches. A useful exercise is to go through results that may be sent to your consultant after a patient's clinic visit.

- **operative surgery**: over the past 3 years, this kind of interactive viva has become an integral part of the oral assessment. The areas that the candidate may expect to be covered include the use of instruments and sutures, common gynaecological operations, as well as the common complications that may be encountered during surgery, such as bladder or bowel injury. Preoperative preparation in the form of a simulated ward round discussion may also be included. On the obstetric side, it may be some form of operative delivery or repair of a complication discovered at the time of delivery.

- **protocol design/audit/risk management**: clinical governance is an essential part of current medical practice. These issues may be addressed by case reviews of problems encountered during a patient's care and a review of how changes could be implemented to prevent similar problems in the future. Clinical governance will usually be addressed in some way, and debriefing a role player after an untoward incident could also achieve this goal. Concerning audit, the process (the audit cycle) is the same irrespective of the topic. It has become mandatory in most units for all the juniors to undertake some form of audit every 6 months. For those candidates who have not previously been exposed to audit, it would be advisable to learn the stages of the audit cycle and to apply it, if this type of question appears.

- **dealing with emergencies**: these emergencies will usually be common problems encountered in clinical practice, including bleeding, fitting or collapse in obstetrics and gynaecology. It is useful for the candidate to have attended at least one of the following: an Advanced Life Support in Obstetrics (ALSO) course, a Management of Obstetric Emergencies and Trauma (MOET) or a local 'drills & skills' session in preparation for this type of station.

- **structured viva**: many topics, in either obstetrics or gynaecology, can be tested in this way, and over the past few years, we have developed a four-part type of question usually dealing with a specific case at different stages of its management. One section leads on to the next but the candidate cannot go back to change their answers. In this kind of viva, equal marks are usually awarded to each part. Actual cases are often used to maintain a realistic feel to the question.

Examiners' briefing

The examiners are fully briefed on the day before the examination and are able to review the questions that they will examine. Each question is discussed and amendments may be made if obvious factual errors have occurred. The examiners are advised not to interact with the candidate apart from initially identifying the candidate in a role-play station. In the interactive viva stations, the examiner will have questions that they will ask and they are advised not to prompt. Some questions may finish before the allotted time and the examiners are instructed to have no further dialogue with the candidate, both candidate and examiner being obliged to endure the uncomfortable silence.

Global score

All the questions will ultimately have a mark out of 20, in total 200 for the whole circuit. In recent years, a global mark has been awarded to reflect the candidate's overall performance and logical approach to a question. The answer/mark sheet cannot be exhaustive and sometimes candidates bring up other relevant information. If this information does not appear on the mark sheet, the examiner has the opportunity of using the global score mechanism to reward the candidate's performance. In some sections of a question where a lot of information needs to be described, a global type scoring system may be adopted. The global score is scored from 0 to 4 (0 = poor, 1 = adequate, 2 = satisfactory/average, 3 = good, 4 = excellent). The role player does not have any influence on this or on any of the marks in a role-playing station.

Standard setting

The pass mark for the examination is derived by a process of standard setting. The examiner awards marks to each candidate but is asked to make an assessment of the candidate irrespective of the actual mark achieved. The candidates are classified as pass, fail or borderline on their performance at a particular station. Some questions are more difficult than others, so the expectation of performance will vary accordingly. For example, one would expect a candidate to score highly on a labour ward board as it is an everyday situation, so the borderline candidate may achieve 13/14 out of 20. A more difficult question, (for example, the use of diathermy) may have a much lower score for the candidates classed as borderline: 8/9 out of 20. The scores of the candidates considered borderline for a question are used to obtain a pass mark for that question and, with 10 stations, the sum of these marks leads to the pass score. The difficulty of the examination may vary between days one and two, so each day may have a different pass mark. At recent diets, the actual pass mark has ranged been between 115and 120. For more on standard setting, see chapter 7.

Logistics of the day

Before the oral assessment you will be sent details of the timing of the examination. You will be expected to register at least 30 minutes before the start of the examination. You will receive a briefing concerning the logistics of the examination, before being taken to your circuit and start station. It is important to take all your belongings with you, as you will be expected to leave the examination centre directly after finishing the examination. If your examination takes place in the morning, the afternoon group will be quarantined while you are leaving the examination centre. This is to avoid any possibility of leaking information concerning the examination to the subsequent group. Similarly, the candidates in Singapore and Hong Kong are quarantined so that no information can be transmitted to them.

On each circuit, the question and candidate's instructions will be pinned to the outside of the station; the same information is available inside the station. When you begin the examination you may peruse the information before the bell goes to start the examination. At that bell, you will enter the station. You may choose to continue to read the question outside but this will reduce the time available for answering the question and, in any case, the same information is available on the table inside the station. If your first station is a preparatory one, enter directly and read through the information. At your first station, you will receive a pencil and notepad, which will be collected at the end of the examination.

The examiner will check your candidate number and you will then have 14 minutes in which to address the question. At the end of 14 minutes, the bell will ring and you will leave that station and proceed in a clockwise direction to the next station. There will be 1 minute for you to read the information of that next station and for the examiners to mark candidates and to undertake the standard setting. There are two preparatory stations and ten interactive stations and so the duration of the examination is 3 hours.

Once the examination is finished, you will be asked to leave the examination centre without delay, taking only what you brought with you, all the examination material remaining the property of the RCOG. The mark sheets are double-checked to ensure that there are no errors in addition.

The numbers game

In recent years, despite the changes in pass marks and the introduction of formal standard setting, a consistent proportion of between 25% and 30% of the candidates sitting the written examination have proceeded to the oral assessment. The pass rate for those sitting the oral assessment and being awarded the MRCOG is usually about 80%. This reflects the fact that most candidates will have the knowledge, experience and ability to pass the oral assessment. Remember that, if you have found a question difficult, it is likely that other candidates will also have done so.

Pitfalls

There are a number of pitfalls for the candidate, although, perhaps surprisingly, lack of knowledge is a minor one. These include:

- **Failure to read the instructions.** This is the major reason that candidates come unstuck, by answering the question they would like to be asked rather than the actual question. The Part 2 Oral Assessment Sub-committee takes great pains to avoid ambiguity and the bullet points that are present in the instructions are the points that will be awarded marks. Usually the marks are distributed equally throughout the sections, unless it is stated otherwise.
- **Poor time management**. Where possible, examiners will ensure that you use the time optimally, although most questions are completed within the 14 minutes allotted. If there are three bullet points in a question, then equal time should be devoted to each section, unless otherwise stated.
- **Poor knowledge of UK practice**. The MRCOG is a British licensing examination, which reflects UK practice. For candidates from outside the UK, practice may be different from that in their country and so it is important to have a good picture of the UK system and its ramifications.

- **Lack of clinical experience**. This is obviously a major reason for failing the examination. The knowledge may be present but its application may be limited, The oral assessment is a clinical OSCE and can only be passed by candidates with clinical skills. This is why the College recommends that it is taken at StR Year 4 or 5.

- **Poor command of English**. Although a candidate's written English may be adequate, they may find difficulty with the spoken word and this may be reflected in slowness in answering questions, misunderstanding of role player's questions and difficulty in the role player's and the examiner's understanding of that candidate's speech.

Preparation

One of the challenging aspects of the Part 2 MRCOG examination is the time lag between the written papers and the oral assessment. It is important that candidates should not lose momentum, and during this time they should ensure that there are no gaps in their knowledge base (the College's comprehensive online distance learning programme, StratOG.net, will be helpful here). History taking practice is important, as these marks should be easy to obtain. Attendance at multidisciplinary team meetings, both obstetric and gynaecological, may prove beneficial in dealing with current practice. Sitting in clinics watching a consultant breaking bad news may also be useful if the candidate has limited experience in that area. There are many oral assessment courses, which may be useful in exposing the candidate to the format and organisation of the circuits.

KEY POINTS

- Anyone who gains a mark in the written paper and proceeds to the oral assessment has a good chance of gaining the Part 2 MRCOG examination.
- Breadth of knowledge and experience is essential.
- The golden rule is to read the question thoroughly.

---

7   Standard setting

Introduction

Standard setting is a process designed to ensure that an examination is fair and equitable, and that the same standard is applied across different examination episodes. In other words, a trainee passing the examination in one year would also pass in a subsequent year. The RCOG introduced standard setting to determine the pass mark of the MRCOG examination in 2002. The standard of the MRCOG is determined by consultants and senior trainees working in clinical practice in the UK. At each standard setting meeting, the process is scrutinised to ensure consistency and fairness. It is vital for the public to have confidence in our postgraduate examination so that women can be assured that those doctors with the MRCOG are practising at a recognised, high standard. Without standard setting, the pass mark of the examination becomes arbitrary or a 'best guess'. Variation in the difficulty or ease of individual questions may inadvertently make an element of the examination more difficult or more straightforward than in previous examination episodes.

How do we set the standard?

There are a number of academically robust methods of setting a standard for the different elements of an examination. The MCQ and EMQ elements of the MRCOG have the standard set using a refinement of the method developed by Angoff. The SAQ paper is standard set by the limen referencing technique and the oral assessment is standard set by a modified Rothman's method, both of which use the concept of contrasting groups. Trained examiners meet before the marking of the written papers to set the standard for all elements of that particular MRCOG examination diet. Standard setting techniques are currently employed for each examination. This ensures consistency and also allows a large number of examiners to be trained in each of the techniques used. Thus, a large proportion of senior members of the specialty are responsible for maintaining the standard required for doctors to become Members of the Royal College of Obstetricians and Gynaecologists.

What happened before standard setting?

Previously, Parts 1 and 2 of the MRCOG examination had fixed pass marks, individual questions varied in difficulty and so the standard of each examination was also subject to variation. Candidates had their papers marked by examiners who were either 'hawks' wanting the pass mark to be high or 'doves' wanting a lower pass mark. Candidates were compared against each other rather than against a defined standard. In other words, the examination was norm referenced rather than criterion referenced. The examination was therefore subjective and open to bias – an increasingly indefensible position for a national 'licensing' examination.

Principles of standard setting

The standard of the examination must be maintained consistently. Cohorts of candidates will differ in ability at each examination but, for the reasons explained, the College must ensure that the same rigorous standard applies whenever the examination occurs. The standard expected applies to all areas of knowledge, skills and attitudes that are to be tested across all parts of MRCOG, as explicitly defined by the curriculum and syllabus.

The consultants trained as examiners are applying their expertise in both setting the examination questions and also the standard required to attain the MRCOG. Standard setting allows us to determine the pass mark for an examination by determining the minimum amount of knowledge or skill required to pass that examination. Examiners are aware of the MRCOG regulations and the content of the curriculum and syllabus, and the standard is set accordingly.

Setting the pass mark requires us to find a method of discriminating between candidates – this is analogous to finding the threshold when the colour orange changes to red in a rainbow. The MRCOG is a high-stakes examination, as further training is dependent on success in this component of the curriculum. The techniques of standard setting are necessary as using the 'mean' of candidates' scores is not acceptable, since it is the area around the mean that we need to explore to define the pass mark for each particular examination diet.

When deciding which standard setting methods to adopt, those responsible for the examination take account of the cohort of candidates being tested and the purpose of the examination.

Angoff method: the MCQ and EMQ papers

The Angoff method is based on the principle of 'probability' or the likelihood of a candidate who is 'minimally competent' answering a question correctly.[1] This requires the examiner to recognise that there is such a person as the 'borderline candidate'. Examiners are asked to imagine a candidate who is of reasonable intelligence, with an average amount of clinical knowledge and who has done a reasonable amount of preparation, and who would be just of the correct standard to pass the examination on that day. With this concept in mind, each examiner is asked to give a score to each MCQ or EMQ question. This score relates to the likelihood that the borderline candidate would know the answer to that particular question. It is emphasised to examiners that they should focus on what the borderline candidate **would** know and not what they **should** know.

The probability of the candidate answering a question correctly can be decided in a number of ways. The probability will be across a range:

Nearly impossible	Possible	Probable	Nearly Certain	Certain
0 1 2	3 4	5 6	7 8	9 10

Using the numerical score based on the above scale, either with percentages or a number between 0 and 10, each question can be given a score. The outcome is that a question that a borderline candidate would find easy will be given a probability score of, for example, 9/10 and a difficult question 1/10.

Another method is for the examiner to imagine a group of ten candidates with a range of abilities; then, for each question, to decide how many of those candidates would answer the question correctly. If, for example, a question was very difficult or 'nearly impossible', the examiner would record a probability of 10% that the borderline candidate would answer correctly. In other words, one in ten candidates would answer correctly.

The scores given for each question of the MCQ or EMQ paper are totalled for each examiner undertaking the standard setting exercise. The calculation to provide the pass mark for each paper takes into account the fact that, where there are true/false MCQs, there can be an element of guessing. To avoid the 'minimally competent' or borderline candidate passing simply by guesswork, this calculation does not simply look at the mean or the median. A combination of these probability scores from a set of examiners gives us the 'pass mark' of each element of the paper. The balancing effect of using a probability approach ensures that a difficult paper will have a lower 'pass mark' than a paper with easier questions.

Limen referencing the SAQ paper

Limen referencing was first described by Christie and Forrest using a concept sourced from information theory.[2] Again, various slight refinements have been introduced since this first description. The word *limen* is derived from the Latin for 'threshold'. This technique relies on the examiners recognising the threshold between a pass and a fail. If we ask the question 'can you tell the difference between red and orange?' the majority of answers will be 'yes'. However, if the question is' can you tell where, in a rainbow, the colour changes from red to orange?' the question is more difficult. By recognising the threshold, we can define the pass mark. We ask examiners to read through a selection of answers from the Part 2 MRCOG written examination. Each group of examiners takes a single SAQ and is asked to decide which papers are clear passes and which are clear fails. Those papers where the examiner cannot decide are placed in a third pile – the borderline group – which plays no part in the subsequent analysis. Subsequently, all the papers are marked by a different set of examiners. These marks are then compared with the papers that are in the pass and fail piles following standard setting, with particular reference to the clustering of marks at the lower end of the 'passes' and at the higher end of the 'fails'. The spread of marks may look like this:

Standard setters 'pass' group	Standard setters 'fail' group
13, 12, 11, 12, 14, 15, 9, 18, 12, 12	7,6,8,10,7,9,9,5,4,7,6
7, 6	13, 14
Threshold	
12, 11	

As is clear, there are outliers in both the standard setting groups, as some examiners will be more generous than others. This is compensated for by having large numbers of examiners mark each question. We are looking for the limits of our ability to perceive success and failure. The examination scripts where it is nor clear whether they are a 'pass' or 'fail' go into a third pile and are of no further use for standard setting. By looking at the difference between these two groups of scores the 'threshold' can be determined and the pass mark set. Obviously each question will have a different pass mark reflecting the relative difficulty or ease of each SAQ.

Standard setting the oral assessment

The oral assessment is standard set using the modified Rothman's method, which uses similar theories and practices to the Limen method.[3] Each examiner at every oral station makes an overall global rating of each candidate's performance (unrelated to their actual mark). The rating divides answers into the same three groups used for the SAQ standard setting: pass, borderline and fail. However, under the modified Rothman's method, owing to its 100% sample of all candidates' performances, a good threshold calculation of the pass mark can be made using the borderline-rated station scores alone and it is this calculation that is used. Again, each oral station has a different pass mark reflecting its difficulty.

STANDARD SETTING KEY POINTS

- The introduction of standard setting for the MRCOG ensures that the examination is a robust, fair and reproducible assessment of doctors in obstetrics and gynaecology.

- It is recognised that the actual pass mark of individual examination components and papers within each diet may vary but the standard will be maintained in a fair and intellectually rigorous manner.

- The RCOG will continue to develop its training of examiners in these standard setting procedures and will ensure that the most up-to-date and appropriate techniques are used.

Blueprinting

The MRCOG examinations are based on an overall blueprint, covering both subjects (such as urogynaecology) and domains (such as management). The blueprint establishes even subject and domain coverage and ensures that examinations are neither too predictable nor unpredictable. In blueprinting, the committee chairs of the various components of the examination confirm the appropriate coverage of the syllabus by a particular examination. Each examination item is categorised by the subject and domain that it is testing, and an overall picture of the entire examination's coverage is thereby revealed. The blueprint systematically outlines an examination's constituent parts, thus ensuring an examination with sound psychometric properties. The blueprint also validates the objectives set by our curricula and syllabuses. In addition, it also greatly assists the planning and review of papers, and the formulation of comprehensive examinations that cover the syllabus in appropriate depth and breadth. The process of blueprinting is derived from a clear, detailed syllabus, which, in turn, is derived from a clear detailed curriculum. Figure 7.1 shows a flowchart representation of this process.

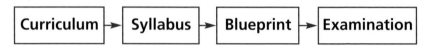

Figure 7.1. Flowchart of the blueprinting process

Since we use blueprints with both a subject and a domain level, these exercises demonstrate the MRCOG examinations' strengths and also highlight those areas that must be addressed through other assessment methods, mainly workplace-based assessments.

References

1. Angoff WH. Scales, norms, and equivalent scores. In: R L Thorndike RL, editor. *Educational Measurement*. 2nd ed. Washington DC: American Council on Education; 1971. p. 508–60.
2. Christie T, Forrest GM. *Defining Public Examination Standards*. London: Macmillan; 1981.
3. Rothman AI, Blackmore D, Cohen R, Reznick R. The consistency and uncertainty in examiners' definitions of pass/fail performance on OSCE (objective structured clinical examination) stations. *Eval Health Prof* 1996;19:118–24.

8   MRCOG: a global examination

Introduction

From a small beginning in 1931, when a handful of candidates were interviewed informally for Membership by Officers of the College, the MRCOG has grown to be seen as the best evidence for competence in obstetrics and gynaecology in over 80 countries. The trend towards international growth shows no sign of slowing and the MRCOG has kept pace, or outpaced, the worldwide growth in medical schools and in the number of graduates. At the time of writing, only 10% of graduating Members of the RCOG work in the UK – the examination and its relevance can be regarded as truly global.

Until recently, we had little understanding of the extent of the dissemination of the Membership examination around the world, nor of the reasons for its popularity. However, the growth in candidate numbers and the diversity in candidate background became so striking that collection of information became imperative and a survey was organised to question candidates to find out more about them and the reasons they were sitting MRCOG. This chapter combines these survey responses with the College's own candidate data, for cross-referencing and to create a rounded picture of candidates and their motivations.

Methodology

The survey was carried out in September 2006. At this diet of the MRCOG examination, 1197 candidates sat the Part 1 MRCOG and 904 candidates took the Part 2 MRCOG examination. A simple questionnaire (Figure 8.1) was given to all the candidates taking the Part 1 and 2 examinations, between the morning and afternoon sessions, and the responses were collected at the end of the examination. Records held by the RCOG of the candidates taking the examination were used for the comparative data. Data analysis was undertaken using simple statistics.

**THIS QUESTIONNAIRE IS ANONYMOUS
IT DOES NOT FORM PART OF THE MRCOG EXAMINATION**

1. Please state your age in years   ....

2. Which is your country of residence?   ....

3. What is your current post?
   - Intern/House Officer   ☐
   - Senior House Officer   ☐
   - Registrar   ☐
   - Consultant in O & G   ☐
   - Other   ☐

4. How many times have you attempted the Part 1/2 examination? ☐

5. If you obtain MRCOG, is your main career aim
   - (i) to work in the United Kingdom   ☐
   - (ii) to work in your country of residence   ☐
   - (iii) to work elsewhere   ☐

6. How important to your career is possession of MRCOG?
   - (i) very   ☐
   - (ii) fairly   ☐
   - (iii) not important   ☐

7. What percentage of trainees in obstetrics and gynaecology working in your institution plan to sit MRCOG examination?
   - (i) almost all   ☐
   - (ii) 50–90%   ☐
   - (iii) 10–50%   ☐
   - (iv) less than 10%   ☐

8. Does your training institution have a programme of workplace-based assessment with
   - (i) a logbook reviewed by a trainer on a regular basis   ☐ Yes ☐ No
   - (ii) annual meetings with trainers to assess progress   ☐ Yes ☐ No
   - (iii) formal assessments of competence carried out in your workplace (e.g. mini-CEX, DOPS)   ☐ Yes ☐ No

9. Please explain why passing MRCOG is important to you (free text):

Thank you for completing this questionnaire. Please bring it to the examination and leave it on your desk for collection. Results will be posted on the RCOG website.

Figure 8.1. Questionnaire designed to find out about MRCOG candidates

Results

Of the 1197 candidates taking the Part 1 examination, 622 (51.9%) responded. The respondents tended to be younger than non-respondents. Among the 904 candidates taking the Part 2 examination, 385 (42.6%) responded and, again, the younger candidates were more likely to respond.

Age of candidates sitting MRCOG

The question regarding the candidates' age was completed by 614 of the 622 (98.9%) Part 1 respondents. The age distribution was 23–53 years, which is a good reflection of the candidates' ages as recorded on the RCOG database, of between 23 and 59 years (only three candidates were above the age of 53 years). The age distribution as seen in the questionnaire is similar to the candidates' records held by the RCOG: 75% of the candidates were between the ages of 25 and 35 years (Figure 8.2).

The question regarding candidate age was answered by 383 of the 385 (99.5%) Part 2 candidates. The age distribution was 28–56 years and the RCOG database showed the age range to be between 27 and 64 years. There were 51 candidates above the age of 50 years. Approximately 70% of candidates sitting for the Part 2 examination were between the ages of 30 and 40 years (Figure 8.3).

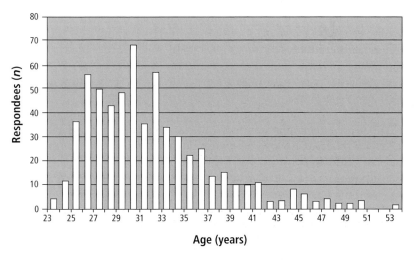

Figure 8.2. Candidate questionnaire: age distribution of Part 1 candidate

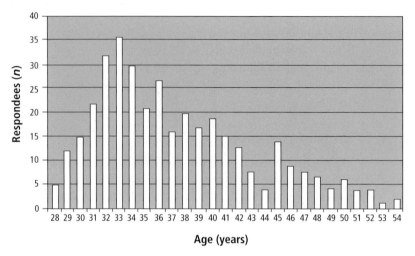

Figure 8.3. Candidate questionnaire: age distribution of Part 2 candidates

Country of residence and of graduation

All Part 1 candidates responded to the question concerning their country of residence. Candidates resided in 46 different countries, having graduated from 69 different countries. The broad geographical, or continental, areas that these fall into are presented in Figure 8.4. Comparing the country of residence with country of graduation revealed a tendency for graduates of Indian, Pakistani and African medical schools to be living and working in the UK and the Middle East; 35% (421) of the candidates were graduates from the Indian subcontinent, 27% (323) from Africa and only 11% (130) from the UK.

Only 28% (174/622) of the Part 1 candidates who responded resided in UK. More surprising was the outflow of graduates from European Union countries to work elsewhere and the influx of non-native graduates into jobs in the West Indies and Asia excluding the Indian subcontinent.

Perhaps the most noteworthy detail of these figures is the fact that the number of MRCOG candidates that have graduated from the Indian subcontinent who are living and working in the UK and the Middle East seemed somewhat less than is commonly believed. A common perception appears to be that candidates with this background and working pattern form the overwhelming majority of candidates for the MRCOG

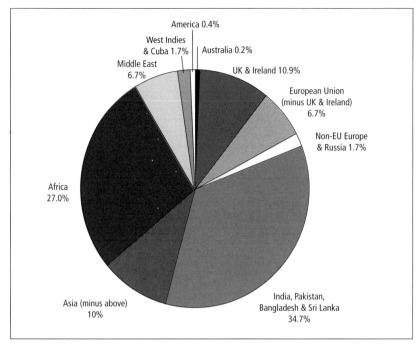

America 0.4%

West Indies & Cuba 1.7%

Australia 0.2%

Middle East 6.7%

UK & Ireland 10.9%

European Union (minus UK & Ireland) 6.7%

Non-EU Europe & Russia 1.7%

Africa 27.0%

India, Pakistan, Bangladesh & Sri Lanka 34.7%

Asia (minus above) 10%

Figure 8.4. Candidates for Part 1 MRCOG by country of graduation

examination. In fact, certainly at the Part 1 level, which will soon feed through to the Part 2 level, the candidate base is far broader, more international and more diverse. This fact and the important implications it carries should be taken into account by employers, supervisors and those offering training for MRCOG when planning for the future. It is now at the forefront of the College's thinking about the examination.

The College records the details of candidates' medical schools. These figures demonstrate the global nature of the MRCOG examination. During the four diets of the Part 1 examination in 2006 and 2007, the candidates were graduates of a remarkable 97 different countries. These countries are listed in Figure 8.5, together with a world map of their location.

Among the Part 2 candidates, 99% completed the question concerning country of residence. Graduates from 56 different countries who were currently residing in 34 different countries took the Part 2 examination. The broad geographical, or continental, areas that these fall into are presented in Figure 8.6; 55% (471) of the candidates had graduated from the Indian subcontinent, 17% from Africa and less

Afghanistan, Albania, Algeria, Armenia, Australia, Austria, Bahrain, Bangladesh, Belgium, Bosnia & Herzegovina, Brazil, Bulgaria, Cameroon, Canada, Chile, China, Croatia, Cuba, Czech Republic, Denmark, Egypt, England, Ethiopia, France, Germany, Ghana, Greece, Grenada, Guyana, Hong Kong, Hungary, Iceland, India, Indonesia, Iraq, Iran, Italy, Jamaica, Japan, Jordan, Kazakhstan, Kenya, Korea (South), Kuwait, Latvia, Lebanon, Libya, Lithuania, Malawi, Malaysia, Malta, Moldova, Montserrat, Morocco, Myanmar, Nepal, Netherlands, Netherlands Antilles, New Zealand, Nigeria, Northern Ireland, Oman, Pakistan, Palestine, Peru, Philippines, Poland, Republic of Ireland, Romania, Russia, Saint Lucia, Saudi Arabia, Senegal, Serbia, Sierra Leone, Singapore, Slovakia, South Africa, Spain, Sri Lanka, Sudan, Switzerland, Syria, Taiwan, Tanzania, Turkey, Turkmenistan, Uganda, Ukraine, United Arab Emirates, United States Of America, Uzbekistan, Venezuela, Wales, Yemen, Yugoslavia, Zambia, Zimbabwe.

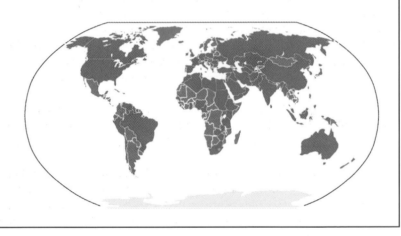

Figure 8.5. Country of graduation of Part 1 MRCOG candidates 2006–07 and marked by the paler grey infill on a world map (Robinson projection; countries with an area under 20 000 km² not marked)

than 5% (42) from the UK. The reduction in the number of Indian and Pakistani graduates sitting Part 1 compared with Part 2 MRCOG is of concern, as it might suggest a reduction in interest in MRCOG in this part of the world. However, the trend can probably be attributed to an atypical 'bulge' in numbers taking Part 2 recently created by the change in regulations for entry to MRCOG from a requirement of a minimum of 2 years of training to one of 4 years in the specialty.

A trend towards more candidates from the Indian subcontinent remaining in their country of graduation is seen among those sitting the Part 2 when compared with the Part 1 candidates. Only 26% (100/

385) of the Part 2 candidates who responded were living in the UK. Although this is only a slightly smaller percentage than at the Part 1 stage (28%), this point stands when the far larger proportion of Indian subcontinent graduates currently in the Part 2 compared with the Part 1 is considered (55% versus 35%).

Chances of passing the MRCOG

Using the RCOG database, we were able to compare the September 2006 examinations with earlier and later diets. Pass rates for the September 2006 examinations were similar to other recent sittings, with a pass rate for Part 1 candidates of 36% (428/1197). More than 80% (365/428) of the candidates who passed the examination did so within their first three attempts; ten (1%) of the candidates had taken the examination more than ten times and there was one candidate who recorded 15 attempts. Pass rates were considerably better for candidates aged less than 35 years. Those of 34 years and under had a pass rate of 38.5%; those aged 35 years and above had a pass rate of 30% (Figures 8.7 and 8.8).

Pass rates for UK graduates were above the mean, at approximately 45% (58/130). This figure is considerably higher than those seen earlier in the decade. For example, in 2003 the pass rate for UK graduates was only 22%. Notwithstanding the improvement in pass rate, the number of UK graduates attempting the examination has fallen dramatically compared with historic numbers in the past few years and constituted only 11% (130) of the candidates in 2006; 35% (143/421) of Indian and Pakistani graduates passed the examination and their pass rate has remained stable over the years.

The chances of passing Part 1 MRCOG in September 2006 were marginally better for the female candidates: a 37% pass rate for women compared with a 33% pass rate for men. At the Part 1 September 2006 sitting, the percentage split of women to men was 79:21.

For the Part 2 MRCOG, the overall pass rate was 25% (221/904). The pass rate for the written examination was 31% (279/904) and for the oral assessment it was 80% (221/277); 80% of the candidates who passed the examination did so in their first three attempts; 8% (71/904) had taken the examination more than ten times and one candidate had 18 attempts. As seen for the Part 1, but rather more strongly, the younger candidates tend to perform better at the examination: 23% (207/904) candidates were between the ages of 41 and 50 years but their pass rate was below 15%. Of the 51 Part 2 candidates who were over the age of 50 years, only two (4%) passed (Figures 8.9 and 8.10).

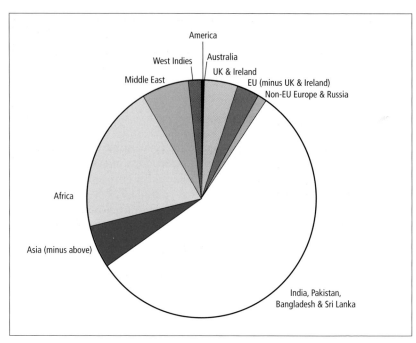

Figure 8.6. Candidates for Part 2 MRCOG, by country of graduation

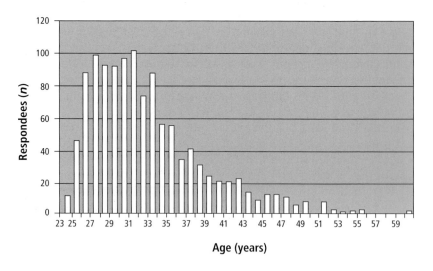

Figure 8.7. Candidates sitting the Part 1 examination, by age

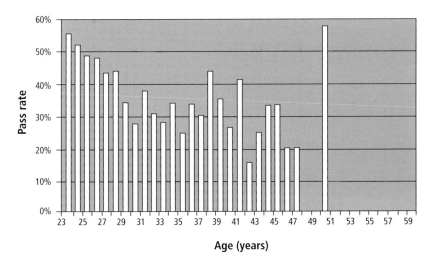

Figure 8.8. Pass rate for the Part 1 examination, by age

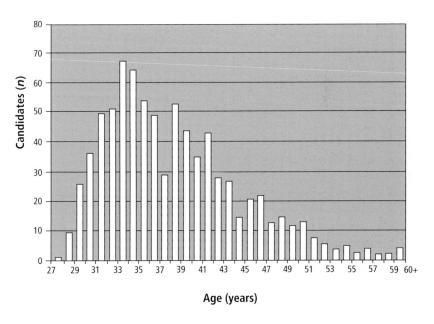

Figure 8.9. Candidates sitting the Part 2 examination, by age

UK graduates constituted less than 5% of all candidates. The pass rate for Indian and Pakistani graduates was 26% (120/471) and they constituted over 50% of the candidates who sat the Part 2 examination. The Part 2 MRCOG has a considerably greater clinical focus than Part 1, with the required standard being that of a Year 5 Specialty Trainee in practice in UK. Given the shortage of training posts and clinical attachments for non-European Union citizens in UK medicine, it is unsurprising that these candidates, who generally have little or no experience of work in a UK setting, perform less well in the Part 2 examination.

Female candidates performed significantly better than their male counterparts at the Part 2 examination, with 29.6% of women gaining a pass compared with 15.6% of men. At the Part 2 September 2006 sitting, the percentage split of women to men was 63:37. This is similar to the distribution seen over the last few years and may reflect the relative lack of attraction of obstetrics and gynaecology to the brighter male candidate; the higher female to male ratio of the Part 1 examination suggests that this is an increasing trend.

Career aspirations and position of MRCOG in clinical training

Among the respondents at Part 1 level, 48% (299/622) planned to work in the UK and 42% (261) wished to work in their country of residence. Only 11% of Part 1 candidates were UK graduates.

At Part 2 level, 38% (146/385) of the respondents planned to work in the UK and 53% (204) of respondents wished to pursue a career in their country of residence. This shift in career aspirations from Part 1 to Part 2 candidates possibly reflects more realistic expectation of future career prospects among the Part 2 candidates.

More than 45% of the Part 1 candidates were working at SHO* level – this is probably the most appropriate point at which to sit Part 1. Seven percent of respondents stated that they were working as consultants. Full details of posts held are shown in Table 8.1.

Fifty-five percent of the candidates taking the Part 2 examination were working at registrar* level, again probably the most appropriate for this stage; 13% of respondents were working as consultants. Full details of posts held are shown in Table 8.2.

---

*   Please note that this survey was completed before the new training grades and terminology in the UK were introduced under the Modernising Medical Careers initiative; it was not thought to be accurate or appropriate to revise these.

Table 8.1. Posts held by candidates sitting Part 1 MRCOG*

Post	Percentage of total
Senior house officer	48.4
Registrar	14.3
Preregistration house officer	10.0
Other	19.7
Consultant	7.0
Intern/house officer	0.3
Unemployed	0.3

Why is MRCOG important to candidates?

The questionnaire contained an enquiry into the reasons behind candidates deciding to sit the MRCOG. Passing the examination requires considerable effort to reach the required level of knowledge. It is also costly, particularly in those countries in which doctors are poorly paid compared with the UK and whose paid currencies have a poor exchange rate against sterling. Overall, 88% of the Part 1 respondents and 81% of the Part 2 respondents considered the examination to be very important for their careers.

Among the Part 1 candidates, 21% of the respondents were taking the examination to achieve promotion or a better job in their country of residence; 45% hoped to pass the examination so as to be allowed to work in the UK and 15% were taking the examination to improve their knowledge. Of the Part 1 respondents, 45% stated that 50–100% of trainees in their hospital were planning to take the MRCOG.

Of the Part 2 respondents, 46% were taking the examination to help with career progression in their country of residence; 35% were planning to work in the UK and 19% wished to increase their knowledge and to keep abreast of newer developments. Forty percent of Part 2 respondents stated that 50–100% of trainees at their hospital intended to take the Part 2 examination.

Table 8.2. Posts held by Part 2 MRCOG candidates*

Post	Percentage of total
Senior house officer	16.8
Registrar	54.9
Other	15.0
Consultant	13.1
Unemployed	0.3

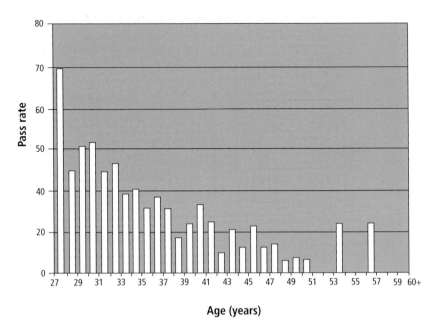

Figure 8.10. Pass rate for the Part 2 examination, by age

Increasing one's knowledge was frequently cited as the reason for taking the examination, possibly a more noble justification than career progression alone. However, many respondents at both Part 1 and Part 2 level believed that possession of the MRCOG would help them to attain a higher professional standing in their chosen field.

Even in the present climate of restriction of entry to UK medical practice for non-European Union citizens, approximately 40% of candidates wished to work in the UK. It is likely that this number will fall as the realities of the new regime of European Union employment law and its implications for the NHS become more widely known in India and Pakistan.

MRCOG and workplace-based assessment

Twenty-three percent of respondents taking the Part 1 examination and 17% of the Part 2 responders stated that they were not involved in any form of workplace-based assessment (WPBA). This reliance on MRCOG alone as a demonstration of clinical competence is at odds with the

RCOG requirement of a pass in the MRCOG examination together with extensive WPBA for a candidate to obtain Certification of Completion of Training in the specialty. Many skills and competencies cannot be adequately assessed in a formal examination setting but can be satisfactorily tested using a variety of workplace-based assessment tools. The quality of non-UK tools for WPBA was not assessed by the questionnaire. It may be that the future development of the MRCOG as a global examination should usefully include development of assessment tools to be made available outside the UK to allow standardisation and quality control of WPBA throughout the RCOG global community. The combination of MRCOG as a test of theoretical knowledge and performance in the oral assessment with high-quality assessment of technical and communication skills in the workplace would be likely to improve the quality of training in obstetrics and gynaecology with a useful contribution to raising the standards of care for women.

Comments in 'free text' from candidates

A selection of quotes from candidates reflects their perception of the MRCOG and its position in clinical training.

- MRCOG is based on good English and 'technique' rather than clinical knowledge and competence. I am wondering how much better an SpR is with or without MRCOG. [UK]
- I want to be called 'Mr' rather than 'Dr'. [UK]
- Allows me to join an elite club of doctors who have attained a higher professional standing in their career. [UK]
- It is one of the highly recognised and well-respected degrees in my country. Preparing for it has made me incorporate the best and evidence based knowledge in my clinical practice. I hope to be a good practitioner for the rest of my life. [India]
- I feel it establishes a minimum standard for those who intend to practise. I feel Part 1 as it stands is mostly irrelevant to today's practice and should be reviewed. However it is important to recognise that as the undergraduate system changes, so will the exam. [Ireland]
- In our country it is important to do MRCOG to continue in this specialty. [Kuwait]
- It is all about keeping one's options open. [Malaysia]
- MRCOG is a window through which I can have more knowledge and find the chance of training in Obs & Gynae. So, it is the step without which I will find difficulty in reaching my goal. [Sudan]

- It would give me the best chance at getting first world training which I could use to advance the level and quality of health care service provided in my country. [Trinidad]
- The United Kingdom is known as Great Britain, so I want to be great as well. [Egypt]
- Passing MRCOG is extremely important for me as it is the most popular & prestigious international exam and in spite of being a good clinician or surgeon passing this exam is like a proof of this. It is like icing on the cake. [India]
- I wish to have an international degree with expertise in evidence-based medicine, audits & protocols, so that I can serve Indian patients better. [India]
- Passing MRCOG is very important to me since I want to attain the best as an obstetrician & gynaecologist. It will give me more recognition. It will also provide me an opportunity to work in the UK. [India]
- I am planning to work away from my country of residence, so MRCOG is the most appropriate & deemed degree in the subject. [India]
- I have almost 5 yrs of experience in O & G, but without the exam I cannot proceed into a career post. It does not at all reflect my experience or abilities in O & G. [UK]
- The Part 1 exam leaves the examinee with a poor impression of the College. The exam is expensive, difficult to pass even with hard work. The question does not feel clinically relevant, but junior doctors are held to ransom by it, as they have to pass to progress in their careers. [UK]
- To get trained in O & G and to become competent in the specialty. [UK]
- It will give me international recognition, and enable me to work in my country or Middle East, where MRCOG is well recognised. The preparation for this exam also gives me an insight into current gynaecological and obstetric practices, especially in the western countries. [UK]
- MRCOG is a prestigious and well-recognised qualification. I wish to attain it for personal satisfaction about the level of my knowledge in the field of O & G. This knowledge in turn will help in serving my people better. [Pakistan]
- MRCOG is an unfair exam for overseas candidates as the majority of those who pass are working in UK, and not everyone can get the

chance to work there. I think it is time to change the system. [Sudan]

- Passing MRCOG is important to me because it means that I have achieved appropriate level to implement RCOG standards to improve women's health. It might in the future also be a gateway that allows me to work in the UK. [Saudi Arabia]

Conclusion

The MRCOG has a relevance to many practitioners in obstetrics and gynaecology worldwide. This global presence presumably dates back to the latter days of the British Empire but this history does not explain its continuing popularity. Our impression of the responses from candidates in 2006 is that many believed that possession of MRCOG would provide them with personal evidence of competence in the specialty. The concept of combining workplace-based assessments with the examination is not universally applied and the RCOG and others should popularise this concept and facilitate its introduction.

It is heartening to know that many candidates are sitting the examination purely to increase their knowledge and to keep abreast of newer developments. However, many candidates for MRCOG who graduate from medical schools outside the European Union still hope to practise medicine in UK. Few will be able to achieve this goal in the current legislative climate and more might be done to disabuse overseas candidates of the notion that MRCOG can guarantee them a job in the UK.

Younger candidates tend to perform much better at both the Part 1 and Part 2 examinations. Although UK graduates do well at the examination, very few of them seem to be taking up the specialty and this is causing a problem in recruitment within UK. When combined with the new immigration regime, this has the potential to grow into a significant damaging 'time bomb' for NHS service provision in the area unless urgently addressed. The lack of attractiveness of obstetrics and gynaecology to male trainees in UK is evidenced by the low numbers of applicants and the low pass rate seen for male candidates. Women's health remains as relevant as ever to the overall health of a country. Death in childbirth and avoidable fetal and neonatal losses are far too common occurrences in many countries. The RCOG, through both the MRCOG and its other educational activities, does much to maintain and raise standards globally. This achievement may be seen as the crowning glory of the College by future generations of obstetricians and gynaecologists.

Appendix 1
Part 1 MRCOG syllabus summary

The Part 1 MRCOG examination covers the basic and applied sciences relevant to the clinical practice of obstetrics and gynaecology. These are summarised here under the modules of the Curriculum. There is inevitably overlap between modules, while at the same time not all subjects and domains are relevant to a particular module. This can be seen in extended form in the syllabus matrix (Appendix 2).

Modules 1, 2, 4 and 19 are not examined by the Part 1 examination

Module 3 Information Technology, Clinical Governance and Research

You should understand the principles of screening, clinical trial design and audit, and the statistical methods used in clinical research. You should know about levels of evidence, quantification of risk, informed consent, and ethical and regulatory approvals in research.

You should demonstrate an understanding of the principles of safe prescribing, quality control in medicine and the accuracy of tests.

Module 5 Core Surgical Skills

You will be expected to demonstrate an understanding of the underlying physiology, pathology and biophysics of basic surgical skills. You should understand the methods of measuring clinically important physiological variables, including the range of imaging techniques. You will be expected to demonstrate knowledge of the genomics, proteomics, physiology and pathology underpinning fluid and electrolyte balance, coagulation, control of blood flow, wound healing, inflammation and immune response, including tissue grafting. You should be able to show understanding of the pathology and epidemiology surrounding surgical complications, including infection and its control and management, and trauma.

Module 6 Postoperative Care

You will be expected to demonstrate knowledge of applied clinical science related to the postoperative period. This will include physiological and biochemical aspects of fluid balance, the metabolism of nutrients after surgery and the biochemistry of enzymes, vitamins and minerals. You should know about the organisms implicated in postoperative infections and be familiar with the antibiotics used to treat them. You should be able to demonstrate knowledge of the other drugs used after surgery, including analgesics and thromboprophylactic agents, and should know the effects of drugs on renal and cardiac function. You should be familiar with the histology of the pelvic organs, the breast and the endocrine organs, including the pituitary and the hypothalamus.

Module 7 Surgical Procedures

You will need to demonstrate detailed knowledge of the surgical anatomy of the pregnant and nonpregnant female. This includes anatomy of the abdomen and pelvis, detailed functional anatomy of bones, joints, muscles, vasculature, lymphatic and nerve supply of pelvic structures, including the genital, urinary and gastrointestinal tracts and of the pelvic floor. You need to demonstrate knowledge of functional anatomy including mechanisms involved in continence, pelvic support and sexual response. You need to demonstrate knowledge of the impact of surgery and anaesthesia on the cells, tissues and organs including body responses to trauma, haemostasis and homeostasis. You also need to demonstrate knowledge of the properties and effects of analgesic and anaesthetic agents.

Module 8 Antenatal Care

You need knowledge of the maternal anatomical adaptations occurring in pregnancy, together with the endocrine and cellular physiology of the major organ systems in both the pregnant and nonpregnant state. You must understand the process of the graft-versus-host reaction and immunological adaptations occurring in pregnancy as well as the underlying immunological processes of infection, anaphylactic and allergy reactions and the effects of immunosuppressive drugs. You need to understand viral biology, infection and infection screening in pregnancy. You also need an understanding of the pathology of lung, renal and cardiac systems, the common haemoglobinopathies and connective tissue disorders. You should be able to define and interpret data on maternal mortality.

You need to understand the development and function of the placenta in pregnancy with a specific knowledge of how the placenta handles drugs.

You should understand the principles of inheritance, the features and effects of common inherited disorders. You need a knowledge of normal fetal physiology and development, together with the aetiology of fetal malformations and growth problems. You should be able to define and interpret data on neonatal and perinatal mortality.

Module 9 Maternal Medicine

You should have an understanding of the pathological processes that underlie common maternal diseases that occur in pregnancy, such as diabetes, endocrine, respiratory, cardiac and haematological disease. In addition, you should know the common infections that affect pregnant women and the treatments that are used. You should have a good knowledge of acid base balance and of the normal ranges of electrolytes in pregnancy.

You should know the drugs that are used to treat maternal disease and the potential maternal and fetal complications associated with their use. You should know about the imaging methods used to screen for maternal and fetal complications of maternal disease, such as ultrasound, X-ray and magnetic resonance imaging.

You should understand fetal and placental growth and development and the immunological adaptations of pregnancy.

Module 10 Management of Labour

You should understand the physiology, biochemistry and endocrinology of the onset of parturition. This will include the maturation of the fetal endocrine system, the influence of hormones on signalling pathways in the myometrium and the biochemistry of myometrial contractility. You should also understand the principles of tocolysis and stimulation of uterine contraction.

You should be able to describe fetal physiology in late pregnancy and you should understand methods for fetal assessment in labour. You should also know about placentation and understand the implications of infection on labour and know the optimal therapeutic options.

Module 11 Management of Delivery

You need a knowledge of the anatomical adaptations of the pelvis and abdomen in late pregnancy and labour and the mechanism and physiology of childbirth and the third stage of labour. You need a knowledge of the aetiology and pathology of congenital and bone malformations of the genital tract.

You need to understand the mode of action of drugs used in labour, at delivery and the third stage of labour.

You need to understand the biochemical basis of acid-base balance.

Module 12 Postpartum Problems

You should be able to demonstrate an understanding of the physiology and structural changes in the neonate. In the mother, you should understand the physiology of lactation, uterine involution and the pathology and management of puerperal sepsis and infection. You should be able to demonstrate an awareness of contraception and other drug use postpartum and during lactation.

Module 13 Gynaecological Problems

You will need to know the anatomy, physiology and histopathology of the pituitary and female reproductive tract. This will include an understanding of changes at puberty, the menopause and during the menstrual cycle including ovulation. You will need to know the microbiology of the organisms present in and introduced into the reproductive tract, the lesions associated and the appropriate treatment. The principles of medical and surgical management of gynaecological problems should be understood.

Module 14 Subfertility

You will be expected to understand the structure (anatomy and development) and function (physiology and cell biology) of the organs of the male and female reproductive tract in context to their relevance to fertility and its disorders.

Module 15 Sexual and Reproductive Health

You will be expected to know about the physiology, endocrinology, epidemiology and pharmacology of contraception. You should demonstrate an understanding of the epidemiology of sexually transmitted infections, the micro-organisms involved, the drugs used their treatment and the pathological features of sexually transmitted disease. You should know about the drugs used in the medical termination of pregnancy.

Module 16 Early Pregnancy Care

You will be expected to demonstrate knowledge of the basic sciences pertaining to early pregnancy and its loss. This will include the endocrine aspects of the maternal recognition of pregnancy, the luteal maintenance of early pregnancy and the physiology of fetomaternal communication. You should have detailed knowledge of the histopathology of intra- and extrauterine pregnancy loss and of trophoblastic disease, as well as of the micro-organisms responsible for pelvic inflammation. You should be familiar with the diagnostic features of ultrasound used in early pregnancy, the epidemiology of pregnancy loss and the medical agents used to manage early pregnancy loss – miscarriage, ectopic pregnancy and trophoblastic disease.

Module 17 Gynaecological Oncology

You will need to know the surgical anatomy of the abdomen and pelvis; understand the genetic origins of cancer and the principles of molecular testing for gynaecological cancer. You should be aware of pain pathways, transmission of pain centrally and the pathology of pain in gynaecological malignancy.

You will need an understanding of the structure, function and regulation of genes, chromosomes, DNA and RNA; an appreciation of cell biology including cell cycle control and carcinogenesis; immunological responses important in gynaecological oncology including tumour surveillance and immunotherapy and an awareness of hormone secreting and hormone-dependent tumours.

You should know the epidemiology of cancers effecting women; aetiological factors, including the role of the human papillomavirus and other viral causes of cancer; the pathology and classification of gynaecological cancer and pre-malignant conditions as well that used for cervical cytology.

You should be aware of the principles of laser and radiotherapy; properties and actions of drugs in the management of gynaecological cancer as well as the affects of chemotherapy on gonadal function.

Module 18 Urogynaecology and Pelvic Floor Problems

You should know the structure of the bladder and pelvic floor and their innervation. You should understand the mechanisms of continence and micturition. You should understand how congenital anomalies, pregnancy and childbirth, disease, infection and estrogen deficiency affect these mechanisms and the impact of drugs on bladder function.

Appendix 2
Part 1 MRCOG curriculum matrix

The Part 1 MRCOG examination covers the basic and applied sciences relevant to the clinical practice of obstetrics and gynaecology. These are summarised here under the modules of the curriculum. There is inevitably overlap between modules, while at the same time not all subjects and domains are relevant to a particular module. If a module or domain is not present, or it is greyed out on this matrix, this denotes that this topic is not examined in this assessment.

Part 1 blueprint

SECTIONS 1 & 2: CELL FUNCTION AND HUMAN STRUCTURE

GLOBAL	UNDERSTANDING CELL FUNCTION			UNDERSTANDING HUMAN STRUCTURE		
MODULE	Physiology	Endocrinology	Biochemistry	Anatomy	Embryology	Genetics
5 Core surgical skills	Principles of fluid and electrolyte and acid-base balance. Methods of measurement of clinically important physiological variables. Physiology of wound healing. Cardiovascular, respiratory, urinary and gastrointestinal physiology. Fluid and electrolyte balance in the perioperative period. Nutritional physiology in health and disease. Blood transfusion. Physiology of liver and nervous system.	Mechanisms of hormone action and second messenger systems. Hormone types. Understanding of hypothalamus, pituitary, pancreas, thyroid and adrenal structure and function. Perioperative care and common endocrinopathies (e.g. diabetes and thyroid disorders). Effects of anaesthesia and surgery on endocrine homeostasis and fluid balance.	Structure and function of normal cell. Proteins, peptides, amino-acids. Catabolism. Nutrition, proteomics, metabolism of proteins, carbohydrates and fats. Biochemistry of enzymes, vitamins and minerals. Cell signalling and second messengers. Effects of surgery on the fetus.	Surgical anatomy of the pelvis and abdomen. Detailed functional anatomy of abdominal wall, abdominal cavity and pelvis, their contents, relevant bones, joints, muscles, blood vessels, lymphatics, nerve supply and histology. Understanding of breast and endocrine gland anatomy. Organisation and structure of the cell and its organelles. Histological appearances of the pelvic organs, breasts, endocrine glands, hypothalamus and pituitary.	Developmental abnormalities in the female. Development of the urogenital tract and structural abnormalities. Structural abnormalities in the female reproductive tract.	Structure and function of chromosomes and genes. Genomics and regulation of gene expression.
6 Postoperative care						
7 Surgical procedures						Diagnosis of fetal anomalies.
8 Antenatal care	Physiology of pregnancy. Fetal physiology and its development with fetal growth. Cellular physiology of the major organ systems in the nonpregnant and pregnant state.	Endocrinology of pregnancy. The placenta as an endocrine gland.	Placental transfer.	Anatomical adaptations to pregnancy. Breast changes in pregnancy. Anatomical interpretation of fetal and maternal images from X-ray, ultrasound and magnetic resonance imaging.	Fetal embryology.	Chromosomal and genetic disorders – principles of inheritance. Features and effects of common inherited disorders and origins of fetal malformation.
9 Maternal medicine	Acid-base, fluid and electrolyte balance in healthy and pathological pregnancy.	Diabetes in pregnancy. Pituitary, thyroid, adrenal and other endocrine disorders relevant to pregnancy.	Cellular biochemistry in disorders of pregnancy.		Fetal and placental growth and development, particularly neural tube, gut and cardiac development.	Screening for fetal anomaly.
10 Management of labour	Physiology of onset of parturition, myometrial contractility and cervical dilatation. Fetal physiology in late pregnancy and during labour, including methods of assessment of fetal wellbeing.	Endocrinology of parturition. Development and maturation of the fetal endocrine system.	Biochemistry of prostaglandins and steroid hormones. Hormones, receptors and intracellular signalling. Biochemistry of myometrial contractility. Second messenger systems.	Obstetric anatomy of the pelvis and abdomen. Changes during late pregnancy and in labour. Mechanism of childbirth.		
11 Management of delivery	Physiology of the third stage of labour.		Acid-base balance.			
12 Postpartum problems	Physiology of the neonate. Lactation and uterine involution.	Endocrinology of lactation.		Structural changes in the newborn.		
13 Gynaecological problems	Physiology of the reproductive tract in women.	Menopause and endocrine effects on bone, vasomotor system, etc. Puberty and growth. Menstrual cycle.		Gynaecological anatomy.	Development of the reproductive tract.	Chromosome abnormalities, single gene disorders, sex-linked inheritance.

GLOBAL	UNDERSTANDING CELL FUNCTION			UNDERSTANDING HUMAN STRUCTURE		
MODULE	Physiology	Endocrinology	Biochemistry	Anatomy	Embryology	Genetics
14 Subfertility	Physiology of the reproductive tract in men and women. Regulation of gametogenesis, fertilisation and establishment of early pregnancy	Endocrinology of the H-P-O axis. Endocrinopathies leading to anovulation in polycystic ovary syndrome, hypogonadal hypogonadism, hyperprolactinaemia and premature ovarian failure.		Anatomy of the hypothalamus and pituitary and the male and female reproductive organs. Surgical anatomy of the pelvis and abdomen.	Development of the gametes, fertilisation, implantation and early embryonic development. Regulation of the embryonic genome. Development of the reproductive tract.	Congenital abnormalities leading to infertility.
15 Sexual and reproductive health	This impact of contraceptives on the phystology of the reproductive tract.	Interactions between hormonal contraceptives and endocrine physiology.				
16 Early pregnancy care	Luteoplacental shift and fetomaternal communication.	Maternal recognition of pregnancy, endocrinology of the corpus luteum and early pregnancy.	Hormonal changes associated with pregnancy loss.		Chromosomal abnormalities associated with pregnancy loss.	
17 Gynaecological oncology	Structure, function and regulation of genes and chromosomes. Abnormal physiology in the genital tract.	Hormone-secreting and hormone-dependent tumours in gynaecology.	Regulation of the cell cycle. Cell biology, including regulation of gene activation, DNA/RNA and cytoplasmic processing. Molecular biology of tumorigenesis and regulation of cell growth and division.	Developmental tumours in the female.		Genetic origins of cancer and DNA mutations. Principles of molecular testing for gynaecological cancers.
18 Urogynaecology and pelvic floor problems	Physiology of the kidney and urinary tract.			Functional anatomy of the pelvic floor, kidney and urinary tract.	Congenital abnormalities of the renal tract.	

SECTIONS 3 & 4: MEASUREMENT, MANIPULATION AND ILLNESS

GLOBAL		UNDERSTANDING MEASUREMENT & MANIUPULATION			UNDERSTANDING ILLNESS		
MODULE		Biophysics	Epidemiology/ statistics	Pharmacology	Immunology	Microbiology	Pathology
3	Information technology, clinical governance and research		Principles of screening. Statistical methods used in clinical research. Principles of clinical trial design. Understand audit cycle and difference to research. Levels of evidence, quantification of risk and chance. Qualitative and quantitative research. Types of clinical trial (multicentre, randomised controlled, etc.). Statistical methods: power of study, level of significance. Understand terms (e.g. confidence intervals, relative risk, odds ratio, attributable fraction). Informed consent. Ethical and regulatory approval.	Safe prescribing, avoiding drug errors, drug interactions, adverse effects. Comparison of effectiveness/cost-effectiveness, number needed to treat.			Quality control, diagnostic accuracy of tests.
5	Core surgical skills	Principles of electrocardiography, ultrasound, Doppler, X-rays and magnetic resonance imaging. Use of laser and electrosurgery.	Epidemiology of surgical complications. Principles of informed consent.	Pharmacokinetics and factors affecting drug action.	Innate and acquired immunity. Organisation of immune system. Cells and humoral elements of adaptive immunity. Immunogenetics and principles of antigen recognition. Hypersensitivity. Immunology of graft rejection and immune responses in infection, inflammation and trauma.	Biology of micro-organisms encountered in surgical practice. Principles of infection control and outbreak management. Biology of micro-organisms in the post surgical patient. Principles of antimicrobial prophylaxis and wound care.	Obtaining and handling tissue for diagnostic tests. Trauma, infection, inflammation and healing of tissues. Effects of radiotherapy, cytotoxics, hormones on tissues. Hyperplasia, neoplasia, atrophy. Disturbance in blood flow, neoangiogenesis, shock, infarction, abnormal coagulation. Renal failure, sepsis (localised and general) e.g. septicaemia.
6	Postoperative care		Factors affecting surgical rates, operative success and complication rates.	Properties and actions of drugs used after surgery: analgesia, thromboprophylaxis, etc. Effects of drugs on renal and cardiac function. Antibiotics and antibiotic prophylaxis. The use of steroids and other drugs in the perioperative period.			
7	Surgical Procedures			Properties and actions of drugs, including anaesthetic agents used during surgery. Effect of drugs on haemostasis and uterine bleeding.			

GLOBAL	UNDERSTANDING MEASUREMENT & MANIUPULATION			UNDERSTANDING ILLNESS		
MODULE	Biophysics	Epidemiology/ statistics	Pharmacology	Immunology	Microbiology	Pathology
8 Antenatal care		Principles of screening. Screening in pregnancy for fetal disorders. Epidemiology of disorders and complications of pregnancy.	Prescribing in pregnancy. Placental handling of drugs. Effects of drugs on the pregnant woman and fetus. Drugs for fetal development and wellbeing.	Maternofetal immunology.	Infection in pregnancy. Screening for infection. Virus biology.	Effect of pregnancy on disease and disease on pregnancy. Teratogenesis.
9 Maternal medicine	Physics of Doppler, ultrasound and magnetic resonance imaging.	Definitions of maternal, neonatal and perinatal mortality and their interpretation.	Drugs and their adverse effects in pregnancy. Drugs used in pregnancy specific pathologies and complications of pregnancy, e.g. antihypertensives and other drugs in pre-eclampsia, steroids in pregnancy, use of anti-D immunoglobulin.	Immunology of pregnancy. The fetus as an allograft. Isoimmunisation.	Infectious complications of pregnancy and their management Fetal impact of maternal infection	Lung, renal, cardiac pathology. Haematological and connective tissue disorders. Immunosuppressive drugs.
10 Management of labour			Tocolysis and stimulants of uterine contractility. Pain relief in labour and the puerperium.		Infection and its management in labour and delivery.	
11 Management of delivery			Drugs in management of delivery. Third stage of labour and its problems. Effects of drugs on the newborn.			Placental site and implantation and its abnormalities (e.g. placenta accreta).
12 Postpartum problems			Contraception in the postpartum period. Use of drugs during lactation. Anti-D and other prophylaxis.		Puerperal sepsis. Infection and its management in the postpartum period.	
13 Gynaecological problems			Drugs in gynaecology, including treatments of menorrhagia, dysmenorrhoea, endometriosis, polycystic ovary syndrome, menopause, osteoporosis and contraception. Effects of drugs on female reproductive system and menstrual function.	Immunology of tissue grafting and graft rejection. Immune responses to infection, inflammation and trauma. Graft versus host reaction, autoimmunity, immunisation and immunosuppression.	Infectious diseases in gynaecological practice.	Congenital abnormalities of genital tract. Osteopenia/ osteoporosis. Pathological conditions of the uterus (endometrium and myometrium), tubes and ovaries.
14 Subfertility	Use of transvaginal and transabdominal ultrasound. X-ray and hysterosalpingography.	Epidemiology of infertility.	Drugs used to treat infertility. Drugs used in anovulation, superovulation and assisted conception. Drug teratogenicity. Drugs that interfere with fertility.	Principles of reproductive immunology.	Pelvic inflammatory disease and its effects on fertility.	Pathology of tubal damage, polycystic ovary syndrome, endometriosis and the pituitary. Histology and pathology of the male genital tract.

GLOBAL	UNDERSTANDING MEASUREMENT & MANIUPULATION			UNDERSTANDING ILLNESS		
MODULE	Biophysics	Epidemiology/ statistics	Pharmacology	Immunology	Microbiology	Pathology
15 Sexual and reproductive health		Epidemiology of contraception and sexually transmitted infections.	Contraceptives. Drugs used for medical termination of pregnancy. Drugs used for sexually transmitted infections, including antimicrobial resistance.		Sexually transmitted infections.	Pathological features of sexually transmitted diseases and female genital infections. Endometrial effects of contraceptive steroids.
16 Early pregnancy care	Ultrasound in early pregnancy.	Epidemiology of pregnancy failure.	Medical management of miscarriage, trophoblastic disease and ectopic pregnancy	Immunology of pregnancy and miscarriage.	Infective factors predisposing to pregnancy loss and ectopic pregnancy.	Pathology of miscarriage, ectopic pregnancy, trophoblastic disease.
17 Gynaecological oncology	Physics of laser and magnetic resonance imaging. Principles of radiotherapy.	Epidemiology of cancers affecting women.	Properties and actions of drugs used to treat gynaecological cancers and trophoblastic disorders. Effects of chemotherapeutic agents on gonadal function. Drugs in the treatment of vulval disease.	Tumour surveillance and immunotherapy.	HPV and other viral origins of cancer.	Pathology, histology, and classification of gynaecological cancers and premalignant conditions. Field change effects. Aetiological factors. Cervical cytology. Pathology of pain and transmission of pain signals centrally.
18 Urogynaecology and pelvic floor problems	Principles of measurement of bladder function.		Properties and actions of drugs used in urogynaecology.		Urinary tract infection.	Pathological conditions of the bladder, urethra and vagina.

Appendix 3
Syllabus for Part 2 MRCOG

Please note that this Syllabus should be read in conjunction with the Curriculum. Modules 4 and 19 will not be examined in the Part 2 MRCOG examination and they do not therefore feature in this Syllabus.

Module 1: Basic Clinical Skills

You will be expected to demonstrate your ability to take an obstetric and gynaecological history, to communicate effectively and to take notes concisely and accurately.

Module 2: Teaching, Appraisal and Assessment

You will be expected to understand the principles of adult learning and to demonstrate aptitude in teaching common practical procedures in obstetrics and gynaecology.

Module 3: Information Technology, Clinical Governance and Research

A. USE OF INFORMATION TECHNOLOGY, AUDIT AND STANDARDS

The examiners will expect you to demonstrate a full understanding of all common usage of computing systems including the principles of data collection, storage, retrieval, analysis and presentation. You will be expected to understand quality improvement and management, and how to perform, interpret and use clinical audit cycles and the production and application of clinical standards, guidelines and care pathways and protocols.

B. RISK MANAGEMENT

You will be expected to demonstrate a working knowledge of the principles of risk management and their relationship to clinical governance and complaints procedures.

C. RESEARCH

You will be expected to understand the difference between audit and research and how to plan a research project but more importantly demonstrate the skills to critically appraise scientific trials and literature.

D. ETHICAL AND LEGAL ISSUES

You will be expected to understand the principles and legal issues surrounding informed consent with particular awareness of the implications for the unborn child, postmortem examinations, consent to surgical procedures including sterilisation, parental consent and Fraser guidelines, medical certification, research and teaching.

E. CONFIDENTIALITY

You will be expected to demonstrate an awareness of the relevant strategies to ensure confidentiality and when it might be broken. You will be expected to understand the role of interpreters and patient advocates.

Module 5: Core Surgical Skills

You will need to demonstrate an understanding of the issues surrounding informed consent. This includes knowledge of the complication rates, risks and likely success rates of different gynaecology operations, together with an understanding of the diagnostic methods and treatment of the complications. You will be expected to demonstrate an understanding of the appropriate use of blood and blood products, together with postoperative fluid and electrolyte balance, and the diagnosis of these different postoperative complications. To show your familiarity with surgery you may be required also to describe the common operations together with common surgical instruments and sutures.

Module 6: Postoperative Care

You will be required to demonstrate an understanding of all aspects of postoperative care – immediate, short-term and long-term. This will include your ability to assess a postoperative patient, know the diagnosis and demonstrate your ability to deal with it. You must know how to prevent common postoperative problems. You will be expected to be able to discuss all aspects of surgery, complications and follow-up with patients and relatives.

Module 7: Surgical Procedures

You will be expected to demonstrate detailed knowledge of the basic surgical procedures performed by a specialty registrar in obstetrics and gynaecology (StR) – including diagnostic laparoscopy, hysteroscopy, gynaecological laparotomy for ovarian cysts, ectopic pregnancy and hysterectomy, and vaginal surgery for prolapse, incontinence and vaginal hysterectomy. You may also be examined on the principles and procedures involved in more complex gynaecological surgery for cancer and endometriosis. You should have good knowledge of the principles of safe surgery, surgical instruments and sutures, and of the management of common complications of surgery. The principles of surgical team-working, risk management and reduction are also important components of this module.

Module 8: Antenatal Care

The examiners will expect a high level of understanding of normal antenatal processes and progress. You will need to be able to recognise and manage problems from preconceptual care through to delivery. Specifically, you should be able to deal with the diversity of maternal choices in antenatal and intrapartum care. You should demonstrate skill in listening and in conveying complex information (such as con-cerning risk). You will need to show understanding of the roles of other professionals and skills in liaison and empathic teamwork. You should be fully conversant with principles of prenatal diagnosis and screening. You should understand the ways in which problems may affect the fetus and should be able to interpret and act on any appropriate investi-gations. You will be expected to have good knowledge of the use of ultrasound and other techniques in investigation and treatment of disorders of the fetus.

Module 9: Maternal Medicine

The examiners will expect you to have a good understanding of common medical disorders and the effect that pregnancy may have on them, and also their effect, in turn, upon the pregnancy. This will include both medical and obstetric problems. You will be expected to demonstrate your ability to assess and treat these conditions, liaise with colleagues in other specialties and to know when more expert help is required.

Modules 10 and 11: Management of Labour and Management of Delivery

The examiners will expect you to have the knowledge, skills, understanding and judgement to be capable of initial management of intrapartum problems without direct supervision. This will include knowledge and understanding of normal and abnormal labour, data and investigation interpretation, clinical judgement and prioritisation, management of a team, communication skills, insights and knowing one's limits, emotional and cultural awareness, and appropriate use of protocols and guidelines. The examination may test certain aspects of practical skill relating to normal or abnormal delivery.

Module 12: Postpartum Problems (The Puerperium)

The examiners will expect you to understand and demonstrate appropriate knowledge, skills and attitudes in relation to postpartum problems. This will include dealing with resuscitation of both mother and baby, as well as demonstrating the ability to manage birth trauma and other birth complications. You will be expected to display empathy, counselling skills and an understanding of the role of other professionals. You should understand and be able to manage neonatal problems at birth, and should be able to discuss these with parents.

Module 13: Gynaecological Problems

You will be expected to demonstrate knowledge of the aetiology, signs, symptoms, investigation and treatment of common gynaecological problems. You should appreciate the influence of psychosocial factors on the presentation and management of these conditions using a patient-centred approach. These gynaecological conditions provide the opportunity for you to demonstrate your understanding of the importance of audit, clinical governance and of taking informed consent.

Module 14: Subfertility

The examiners will expect you to demonstrate appropriate knowledge, skills and attitudes in relation to subfertility. This includes an understanding of the epidemiology, aetiology, pathogenesis, clinical treatment and prognosis of all aspects of male and female fertility problems. Your knowledge will include indications, limitations and interpretation of relative investigations and treatments in relation to both male and female including disorders of development and endometriosis. You will be expected to have a broad based knowledge of assisted reproductive techniques including: ovulation induction, in vitro fertilisation and intracytoplasmic sperm injection, gamete donation, surrogacy and the legal and ethical implications of these procedures.

Module 15: Women's Sexual and Reproductive Health

You will be expected to demonstrate appropriate knowledge, skills and attitudes in relation to fertility control, the diagnosis and management of sexually transmitted infections, including HIV and sexual dysfunction. In particular, you will be familiar with irreversible and emergency contraception and abortion, their modes of action, efficacy, indications, contraindications and complications. You should be familiar with the accompanying laws related to abortion, sexually transmitted disease, infection, consent and child protection. You will need to demonstrate a broad based recognition of management techniques relating to the sexual health of vulnerable groups such as young people, asylum seekers, commercial sex workers, drug users and prisoners. You will also be expected to know the basis of national screening programmes and their implementation through local care pathways.

Module 16: Early Pregnancy Care

The examiners will expect you to have a good understanding of early pregnancy and pregnancy loss. This will include the diagnosis, investigations, management and psychological support in miscarriage and ectopic pregnancy. You will be expected to be able to assess and manage these conditions both medically and surgically, and also to demonstrate your abilities to communicate the relevant information to the patient. It will be essential for you to have knowledge of the use of ultrasound in both the diagnosis and management.

Module 17: Gynaecological Oncology

You will be expected to have full knowledge of the aetiology and screening involved in gynaecological oncology, including the international perspective. An understanding of presenting symptoms and their management is required together with the appropriate competencies for each stage of the diagnostic process to include a comprehension of the different roles and skills required in district lead and gynaecological oncologist. Knowledge of the prognosis and treatment options of the gynaecological cancers is necessary, and you may be asked to demonstrate your ability to provide counselling for women with gynaecological cancer.

Module 18: Urogynaecology and Pelvic Floor Problems

You will be expected to understand the management of urinary and faecal incontinence, benign bladder conditions and urogenital prolapse. The examiners will expect you to demonstrate an understanding of the anatomy, pathophysiology, epidemiology, aetiology and investigation of these conditions. You should know when more experienced help is required in the management of your patients, and you must be able to discuss clearly all aspects of management with patients, carers and other continence providers.

Examination Committee
May 2007

Appendix 4
Part 2 MRCOG examination analysis

Division of marks

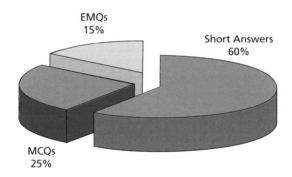

EMQs
15%

Short Answers
60%

MCQs
25%

Lengths and question numbers of papers

PAPER	EMQ & MCQ
Length	One 2¾-hour paper (165 minutes)
Question numbers	40 EMQ questions; 225 MCQ questions
Timing advice	Candidates are responsible for their own time management. However, our recommendation is that candidates should spend 75 minutes on the EMQ questions and 90 minutes on the MCQ questions
PAPER	SAQ
Length	Two papers; each of 1¾ hours (105 minutes)
Question numbers	8 Questions overall (4 in each paper)

SUMMARY OF THE MARKING SCHEME

The written examination is marked out of 425.

MCQ	225	Marked by computer
EMQ	40	Marked by computer
SAQ	160	Marked by examiners

A Pass in the written paper is required in order to proceed to the oral assessment

The oral examination is marked out of 200.

Appendix 5
Administrative practicalities: a guide for candidates

The following practical information is included as an aid to candidates preparing to sit the MRCOG examination. Some of the points will seem obvious but they are intended to reduce some of the anxiety surrounding the sitting of a high-stakes postgraduate examination.

Please ensure that all application forms are completed carefully, in line with the Membership Examination Regulations and Frequently Asked Questions (FAQs) available on the College website (www.rcog.org.uk). Ensure that application forms arrive in London by the relevant closing date. Owing to the large number of candidates and the large number of MRCOG examination centres, all closing dates are firm and final. They cannot be extended, whatever the extenuating circumstances. Certificates sent in support of applications should be sent via a secure method; we therefore recommend the use of attested copies to eliminate the possibility of their loss. Full examination fees must accompany applications. Please note that the College does not accept bank transfers.

Make arrangements for obtaining visas to attend examination centres, if applicable, as early as possible. Please contact the relevant consulate to obtain information concerning the visa requirements **before** applying for the examination. The College is unable to offer advice regarding visas. If you require a letter from the Examination Department confirming your attendance at the examination, please inform us of this when applying for the examination and ensure that you apply in good time. It will be sent with your acknowledgement letter and receipt in due course.

Please allow plenty of time to travel to your examination venue. Arriving in good time will reduce your stress levels considerably. Candidates will not be allowed to enter the examination hall after 30 minutes have elapsed from the starting time. However, arriving even 10 minutes late may well seriously damage your chances of success. Refunds are not granted to latecomers. Late attendance at any stage of an examination may result in failure of the entire examination.

Candidates must bring evidence of identification, which includes their name and photograph, to all sections of the Part 1 and Part 2 Membership examinations for scrutiny by the invigilators and examiners. Candidates who fail to produce satisfactory identification at the beginning of any section of the examination will normally be refused entry to that examination.

Please note that candidates are not allowed to leave the examination hall until 1 hour after the commencement of each paper or during the final 10 minutes. This is to minimise disruption to other candidates, although of course you should always leave very quietly. Two time warnings will be given: the first at 30 minutes and the second at 10 minutes before the end of each paper. Candidates must stop writing immediately when advised by the invigilator; failure to comply with this regulation may result in disqualification. Invigilators are instructed not to discuss questions with candidates during the examination.

There is no time limit between passing the Part 1 and passing the Part 2 MRCOG examination. However, the Regulations require you to have **attempted** the Part 2 at least once within 10 years of passing the Part 1. You do not have to **pass** the Part 2 within 10 years of your Part 1 pass but, if you do not even attempt it, you will be required to pass the Part 1 examination again.

After passing the Part 2 written examination, candidates must appear for the immediately succeeding oral assessment. The reason for this is that both components are organised, written and blueprinted as a unified whole. Candidates must take this fact into account when making their work and travel plans. A pass in the Part 2 written examination cannot be carried over to a future examination diet. If you do not appear at the immediately succeeding oral assessment (or if you fail it), you will need to resit the Part 2 written examination. However, your performance in the Part 2 written examination does not affect your score in the succeeding oral assessment: the two components are marked independently. Only the MRCOG Prize Medal is awarded on the basis of a combined score.

EMQ and MCQ papers: general information

The EMQ and MCQ papers of both Part 1 and Part 2 must be completed using only pencil. Pencils and erasers are provided by the College. Please do not use pens of any sort, as they cannot be read by the computerised optical scanners. Even propelling pencils cannot be used, as they can create indentations or tears in the answer sheets that can jam the scanners. Similarly, answer sheets must not be folded, creased or torn.

Please print your name as stated on your entry slip at the top of the answer sheet and write your **four-digit candidate number** (**not** your desk number) in the boxes provided. Then **black out** the lozenges corresponding to your candidate number (as shown in the example in Figure A5.1).

At the end of the examination, insert the completed answer sheets inside the front cover of the question book.

Front cover: On the front cover of each question booklet, please print your name in the boxes provided and then sign your name in the space marked 'signature'. Your candidate number must also be written in the four squares provided.

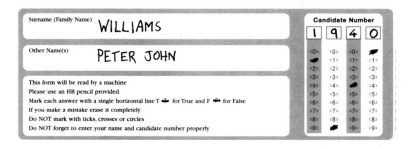

Figure A5.1. Black out the lozenges corresponding to your candidate number

EMQ sections/paper

ANSWERING THE QUESTIONS

The answer sheet is numbered 1–20 for the Part 1 EMQ section and 1–40 for the Part 2 EMQ Paper. Against each number there are 20 lozenges labelled from A to T. Each question in the question booklet will consist of an option list (lettered to reflect the answer sheet), a lead-in statement (which tells you clearly what to do) and then a list of one to five questions (each numbered, again to match the answer sheet). Indicate your judgment of each particular question by **boldly** blacking out the letter that corresponds to the single best answer in the option list. Candidates may choose to mark their responses in the question booklet and then transfer these to the answer sheet. However, please be aware that this will take longer and all transfers **must** be completed fully **within** the time allocated for the examination.

Although the answer sheet will provide 20 possible answers, the option lists for questions may not use all of these. Most option lists will provide 10–14 answer options.

SPECIMEN ANSWER SHEET

A portion of a completed answer sheet may look like the example in Figure A5.2.

⊏G⊐ ⊏H⊐ ⊏I⊐ ⊏J⊐ ⊏K⊐ ⊏L⊐ ⊏M⊐
⊏G⊐ ⊏H⊐ ⊏I⊐ ⊏J⊐ ⊏K⊐ ⊏L⊐ ⊏M⊐
⊏G⊐ ⊏H⊐ ⊏I⊐ ⊏J⊐ ⊏K⊐ ⊏L⊐ ⊏M⊐
⊏G⊐ ⊏H⊐ ◀▶ ⊏J⊐ ⊏K⊐ ⊏L⊐ ⊏M⊐
⊏G⊐ ⊏H⊐ ◀▶ ⊏J⊐ ⊏K⊐ ⊏L⊐ ⊏M⊐

Figure A5.2. A portion of a completed answer sheet

MCQ sections/paper

ANSWERING THE QUESTIONS

The Part 1 MCQ section of the answer sheet is numbered 21–68 and each question number has five components, lettered A to E. Against each letter there are two lozenges labelled T (= True) and F (= False).

The Part 2 MCQ paper answer sheet is numbered 1–225 and questions are not divided into specific components. Each stem may have between one and five components. Against each letter there are two lozenges labelled T (= True) and F (= False).

A	B	C	D	E
T ▮	T ▮	T ▮	T ▮	T ▮
F ☐	F ☐	F ☐	F ☐	F ☐

Figure A5.3. A Part 1 specimen answer sheet

For both papers, indicate your judgment of each particular question by **boldly** blacking out either the T or F lozenge. Candidates may mark their responses in the question book and then transfer these to the answer sheet. However, please be aware that this will take longer and all transfers **must** be completed fully **within** the time allocated for the examination.

A Part 1 specimen answer sheet is shown in Figure A5.3 and a Part 2 specimen answer sheet in Figure A5.4. In both, 'T' means 'TRUE' and 'F' means 'FALSE'.

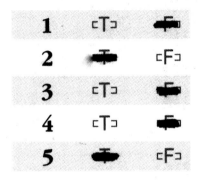

Figure A5.4. A Part 2 specimen answer sheet

Part 2 SAQ papers

The Part 2 SAQ papers are completed in pen in black or blue ink. Please feel free to bring your most comfortable, legible and easy-to-use varieties of these. Short Answer Paper 1 contains four SAQs numbered 1–4; all questions must be answered. Short Answer Paper 2 contains four SAQs numbered 5–8; all questions must be answered.

Please ensure that your candidate number is written in the space provided on <u>each</u> of the <u>eight</u> short answer questions/ answer sheets. Each SAQ is marked out of 20. Each question and answer space is now clearly subdivided. **Only answers in the correct space for each sub-question will gain marks.** Do **not** stray out of these areas (that is, do **not** run on an answer into the next space or link to a different area with an arrow). Replacement booklets, answer sheets or additional rough paper will not be provided for answering the SAQ questions.

Index